April 2017

To Erica:

So many memories –
So much gratitude!

With love
Gina + Gail

hasten slowly

LESSONS FROM THE HIMALAYA

1987 - 2012

GORDON and GAIL KONANTZ

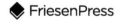 FriesenPress

Suite 300 - 990 Fort St
Victoria, BC, V8V 3K2
Canada

www.friesenpress.com

ISBN
978-1-4602-8392-9 (Hardcover)
978-1-4602-8393-6 (Paperback)
978-1-4602-8394-3 (eBook)

1. TRAVEL, ASIA, INDIA

Distributed to the trade by The Ingram Book Company

Hasten slowly, or *festina lente* seems to be a contradiction, but this advice dates back to the time of the Emperor Augustus. In the 15th century La Fontaine wrote in his famous Hare and Tortoise fable that the tortoise achieved his goal and "with a prudent wisdom hastened slowly".

Our goal while travelling with Everest Trekking Canada has been to broaden our minds as much as to seek adventure. Distraction, the scourge of modern life through computer screens, social media and cell phones, makes us available to everyone but ourselves. Hasten slowly is the opportunity to look inward, and leave distraction behind. Thus our title and the wisdom we gathered along the way as we learned our lessons from the Himalaya.

preface

GORD

*All the great travel books are love stories, and all good trips are
like love, about being carried out of yourself and deposited
in the midst of terror and wonder.*

– PICO IYER

My love of the outdoors was evident as a boy growing up in Winnipeg. On the coldest winter days, I loved being out in the yard in my snowsuit, feeling the bite of Arctic air against my face. I could spend hours making caves in the snowbank across the street from my house in Assiniboine Park. I played shinny hockey constantly with friends at the outdoor rink in our neighbourhood. To travel with my parents to La Rivière, a rift in the prairie floor, for a weekend of skiing was an adventure I looked forward to all week. I still feel the excitement I felt then as I waxed my skis in the foyer of the Barclay House Hotel and then herringboned up Station Hill with my breath forming icicles on my scarf. We would ski through the scrub oaks and bush to the edge of the Crows Nest, or MacCoubrey run, and gaze in anticipation at the valley all of 60 metres below. The uphill lift was a basic rope tow; the shelter a small shed heated by a coal burning stove.

This was the limit of my world until I discovered *Kingdom of Adventure: Everest* written by James Ramsay Ullman. Published in 1947, this book was Ullman's chronicle of man's assault on the earth's highest mountain as narrated by the participants. Only six years later, Ed Hillary and Tenzing Norgay would successfully summit Everest, but it would take me close to fifty years before I reached the base of the mountain to see it with my own eyes.

Here was a book to ignite the imagination of a young boy living on the prairies in Canada. Everest and the Himalaya became indelibly etched into my imagination and dreams. This book is the story of our many journeys to the world's highest mountain range. I am now 83. My most recent trek in Nepal was four years ago. It was my thirtieth visit to the mountains of Nepal and Bhutan.

I sit in my study in Vancouver, a small room bursting with books related to the Himalaya, personal journals, National Geographic magazines devoted to Mount Everest, an ice axe signed by Sir Edmund Hillary, photos, maps, yak bells, thangkas, Buddha sculptures, memorabilia, files, and gifts. It is the repository of our memories over the last twenty-five years.

Little did my wife Gail and I know that in 1987 our lives would change so dramatically, when we first stepped through the looking glass into a land and culture far from anything we had ever known.

inside

Preface 4

Introduction 8

Everest Through Innocent Eyes 12

The Annapurna Circuit 30

Sherpa Friends Of Namche Bazar 38

Leadership Challenged 46

Lost On Annapurna 52

Climbing High With The Nomads 56

The "Oh My God" Group 60

Jewelweed And Elephants 66

Tibet 78

Mustang 90

Kopan Oms and Copra Ridge 96

Solu 100

Bhutan 108

Khumbu Coughs And The Renjo La 116

Close Call On The Manaslu Circuit 120

Setbacks And Solutions 126

Bistarai Ja-nay 138

Himalayan Moments 142

introduction

GORD

We moved to Vancouver from Winnipeg in October 1986, and early in January the next year departed for an extended Asian tour. We cycled in New Zealand and Bali, sailed in the Whitsunday Islands in Australia, and rode elephants in northern Thailand. In early April we landed in Nepal to begin a three-week trek to the Everest Base Camp.

This was our first trip to Asia, and the first time we had seen a country like Nepal. We had signed on to a high-end program with Sobek Travel of San Francisco and found that only the two of us and two other clients comprised the group. Because of the small number, and without our knowing the difference, the company replaced the western trek leader with a Sherpa who had limited English language skills. We were about to discover how this compounded the problems involved with taking groups of foreign travellers to a high altitude.

On our return to Vancouver, we both agreed that Nepal was the highlight of our Asian adventure. We felt we had to return with friends and family so they could appreciate both the mountains and the people of that beautiful land. There were lessons to be learned, trails to explore, people to meet and ideas to discover. This love of travel and of mountains was to lead to the beginnings of our adventure travel business.

Our first task was to find a resident of Kathmandu to act as a trusted partner for the complicated arrangements required for trekking in remote mountains. This was not mountain climbing, but walking on the timeless trails used by local villagers and their animals. These trails crossed valleys and passes in the most economical ways. To us the scenery was breathtaking, and the opportunity to walk through villages, meet local people, and absorb a different culture was compelling.

Through a referral from a close friend we contacted Tashi Sherpa of Kathmandu. Tashi, a multi-lingual certified mountain guide, looked like the perfect choice. In November of 1988 I wrote to him with a trekking business proposal. Surface mail to Nepal was the only way to communicate at that time. There was no way to reach him by telephone or fax. Knowing it would take about six weeks for the letter to turn around, I paused, aware that this was a watershed moment before dropping the envelope in the mailbox.

Six weeks later, an envelope arrived from Tashi at Everest Trekking Nepal. The proposal was organized and complete.

With Tashi, we created the ideal partnership. As he was known as Everest Trekking Nepal, we would use the name Everest Trekking Canada. Our adventure travel company would be designed to appeal to mountain-loving people over fifty, in our age range, who were looking for guided walking tours in the Himalaya. Quality and safety were our priority, backed up by the best possible staff, food, and equipment. In addition, air travel to and from the trailhead would be included whenever possible. Price was secondary. To complete the circle of service, Henry Oyoung and his travel team at Richmond Travel in Richmond, BC provided us with superb trans-Pacific air routes into Kathmandu, and later to Hanoi, Delhi, Paro and Yangon.

When travel to Nepal became difficult in 2001, we expanded our horizon to include Bhutan, India, and Indochina. We remained a small and personal operation. Our trek leaders were our friends; our market was essentially Canada. We partnered with several ground operators in Asia who met our quality criteria. For twenty-five years, we have guided over seven hundred people, high and low, far and wide. With few exceptions, our clients have been goal-oriented, success-driven individuals. All the squares in their calendars were filled for a year or more ahead. Watching the local mountain dwellers, we quickly learned that health and happiness started with a slow and steady walking pace; that rushing often led to physical breakdown; and that altitude was won only by patience.

One of the first Nepali phrases we learned was Bistarai Ja-nay – "Go slowly". It became our daily mantra, and we made it an important change for our clients who invariably began at a dash. It was fun to watch as their mental files faded, watches were removed, and their senses expanded to impress them with the deep pleasure of living right now rather than projecting thoughts and plans into next week. The exhilaration of a day on the trail was paramount. Bistarai Ja-nay became the first lesson learned.

This story is about the many lessons learned during our travels, both by us and by our western clients and friends, the knowledge and perspective we gained, and the fascinating people we met along the way. Here were adventures suffused with wonder, fear, exhilaration, exhaustion, accomplishment, and love.

Over forty times combined, the two of us have stepped onto the tarmac at the Kathmandu airport. Friends have asked why we wanted to go back. Sharing our tales, we hope you will see why we love this country and never tire of travelling among the world's most majestic mountains.

People signed up for our Himalayan treks for many reasons. Curiosity, adventure, and a sense of accomplishment usually headed the list. Other reasons were more obscure. Some were at a crossroads in life; others were openly searching for the "something more" to enrich their days. While everyone was astounded by the humbling vastness of the mountain landscape, few anticipated the powerful effect the people would have on them. In spite of vast differences in material wealth, they discovered that less is often more, that happiness derived from spiritual appreciation trumps attachment to possessions and that comfort was a relative term.

To witness these truths as they became evident to our first-time travellers was, for us, a profound reward.

> HERE WERE ADVENTURES SUFFUSED WITH WONDER, FEAR, EXHILARATION, EXHAUSTION, ACCOMPLISHMENT AND LOVE.

Tashi Sherpa

Henry Oyoung & the Richmond Travel wizards

chapter 1

EVEREST THROUGH INNOCENT EYES

1987 | GAIL

Kala Pattar, 5,554 metres

We were flying at 10,000 metres into the dusky light above Kathmandu. It was moments before nightfall as, level with the sun-touched peaks, we began our descent into the darkness below. The few electric lights belied the fact that 300,000 people lived in this valley. A dingy, ill-lit airport structure greeted us. Signs painted by hand, partially obliterated, directed us to customs and beyond to the foreigners' exit. We entered a small waiting room where a blackboard listed hotels. The M and M hotel looked practical because it was in Thamel, where we had been advised to spend what was left of the night. After we fought our way through the porters in the ticket area, a driver grabbed our bags and ushered us into a decrepit Toyota. Bumping along dirt roads and paths in the dark for what seemed like hours, we finally arrived at our destination – a shabby, run-down hostel. Our room featured a rock-hard bed, a red carpet splotched with years of lurid stains, and thankfully, a western toilet, something we have never taken for granted.

A short walk around the dusty roads in the area the next morning impressed upon us the poverty of this country. People looked grimy, and everywhere dirt and garbage confronted us. Now and then a couple of rats feasted brazenly in the middle of the narrow road we shared with food carts, rickshaws, beggars, and other tourists. We were on our way to the recommended Kathmandu Guest House to book a better room. The lobby was a bustle of activity, with tours being organized and trekkers surrounding the one phone by a booking desk. Such energy, excitement, and pleasant surroundings made us feel welcome.

The next afternoon we rented bikes and got lost while looking for a bookstore that sold maps. All the street stalls were aglow with colour, and alleys were jammed with rickshaws, cars, bikes, and crowds of people. Everywhere, the streets were littered with jumbles of metal – patched, bent, rusted, or with missing parts. We cycled through parts of town that were filthy with flies, dead dogs, and dismembered

cows – legs and other body parts rotting in the sun. We held our breath for fear of breathing in disease. This was a long way from our Western society, obsessed with cleanliness.

It was challenging to relate this reality to the book we had recently read called Magical Kathmandu. We continued on to the Swayambhu temple, high on a hill where the all-knowing eye of Buddha gazed in the four directions of the valley. Hindu and Buddhist religions intermingled here. The iconography differed, but the message was similar. Life is a wheel without a beginning or ending, and it is important to live it virtuously.

We had a room with a hot shower at $13 a night, but for the local people, running sores, chronic coughs, and polluted water seemed commonplace. Lack of sanitation affected us too, as we both were feeling increasingly queasy. The next day we moved to the more luxurious but less charming Sheraton Hotel to meet our fellow trekkers and tour company officials. We wrote postcards by the pool while sensing the penetrating eyes of a gaggle of Nepalese boys. They stood on a nearby rooftop and gawked at us through a wire mesh fence. The chasm between us was palpable; impossibly rich tourists lounging around an aquamarine pool and kids who would so love to change places with us. Hem, our sirdar, met us along with Lock, a bank clerk from Melbourne, and Cyril, a road grader and snowplow operator from Canada. They would be our only travelling companions. Now we discovered that the group was so small that the company had considered cancelling our trek. Instead, they cut staff, shortened days, and gave us a local guide as a sirdar, who spoke marginal English. The sirdar is the primary liaison between the client and the staff. He does all the organizing, hiring, and firing of staff, and makes sure things run smoothly each day. He carries a first-aid kit. He also decides where campsites should be and how far to walk in inclement weather.

At dawn the following morning, feeling ragged and suffering from diarrhea, we piled into an ancient bus along with a crowd of Nepalese who had signed on to be our staff. With our baggage lashed to the roof, we rattled off down the road, eastbound to the trailhead. All morning, we passed crowded buses with people perched on the roof and squeezed between open windows. After lunch we crossed a river on a narrow bridge built by the Chinese. Then we began the tortuous climbs and descents around and down steep, narrow valleys and terraced slopes on a road barely wide enough for us, but sturdily engineered by the Swiss government, but barely wide enough for us.

Several times I gulped and gagged as the road narrowed, and one back wheel disappeared over the chasm. The driver's muscles flexed time and again as his hands pushed and pulled the wheel to steer – now clockwise, now counter-clockwise. I felt sick from the smell of gasoline sloshing over the top of the can resting between the knees of the man in front of me. We watched in horror as he stamped out sparks from the cigarette he had just lit. There were twenty men on the bus, and I was the lone female. We four travellers required an army of seventeen porters to carry our tents, gear, food, and cooking equipment over the mountains.

Clouds formed, spilling down the hills, and before long a driving rain obscured all but the road directly in front of us. With the deteriorating weather came the cold and a sinking depression. We had been on this bus for nine hours by the time Jiri appeared in the faint evening light. Figures enshrouded in rags to stave off the rain surrounded the vehicle when it stopped and helped our staff shift sacks and bundles from the roof rack into the gloom of the 12th-century inn. We were disgorged into a sea of mud to join these rags in the rain.

Our lodging was a two-story shed. Firewood was stacked in the front hall along with a confusion of oil

Namche Bazar

WE HAD LEFT THE 20TH CENTURY AND
FOUND OURSELVES IN A BRUEGHEL
PAINTING WITH FIRES LIT ON EARTHEN
FLOORS AND SMOKE SEEPING THROUGH
MAKESHIFT ROOFS.

drums, sacks, cases, pots, and ropes. We had left the 20th century and found ourselves in a Brueghel painting, with fires lit on earthen floors and smoke seeping through makeshift roofs. Huge baskets of equipment, fuel, pots, and gear were passed from the roof of the bus to the dry inside hall as we were led up a slippery wooden staircase outside the structure to our second-floor room. We found ourselves in a cubicle with peeling whitewashed walls and two hard beds. The door had an enormous iron padlock. A small electric bulb in the ceiling throbbed weakly, accentuating the dingy atmosphere. Two monks chanted in the cell across the hall.

Dinner was cooked by our kitchen staff in a room below that passed for a kitchen, and served in our travel companions' room. We sat on their beds and ate from a table between us. The food was delicious: soup with lentils, rice, cauliflower and carrots, and potatoes with yak meat. Half an orange and tea concluded the feast, and we were warmed and feeling less depressed.

I ventured to the bathroom, down the outdoor steps and into the main entrance to ask for a key. Outside the building at the back, I found a three-sided structure with Toilet 1, Toilet 2, and Toilet 3 penned on the doors. I had the key to Toilet 2, and opening the door, I discovered a not-too-clean concrete foot platform with a hole in the floor. I was going to do anything to avoid repeating that trip during the night.

Back in our room, we prepared our sleeping bags for bed and tried to sleep. Downstairs, people played cards around a fire, talking and occasionally shouting while the smoke curled up through the gaps in the floorboards and caught in our throats. Above us a child coughed while dogs barked incessantly outside the window. By 10:30, as if on a command, all was quiet, and we slept until a soft knock on our door at six announced the arrival of morning tea and wash water. Breakfast between the beds consisted of muesli, pancakes, fried eggs, toast, and tea. We packed our bags and a porter carried them away.

Outside, baskets overflowing with food, folding chairs, and pots and pans were being secured with ropes threaded through the lattice. A tumpline was placed over the squatting porter's forehead, while another porter pushed him up into a standing position. Slowly they moved off, disappearing into the mist at the end of the street and began their journey into the mountains. Along the route, crowds of porters descended, their baskets empty. Some were sitting by the trail, devouring breakfasts of dal bhaat sprinkled with nettles found along the trail. This complex protein, rice and lentils, formed the perfect energy-producing base for their diet. Others rested loads on their ubiquitous T-shaped walking sticks called tokmas. Farmers worked at every level in steep terraced fields, tending crops and goats, while women sat by the path nursing their babies.

Arriving at the top of a hill accompanied by Mingma, our Sherpa and chief guide, we found that lunch had been prepared in a broad field high above the valley. The cook staff always managed to set up a camp kitchen ahead of our arrival. It was only midmorning, but along came tea, potatoes, pancakes, and tinned meat. We weren't even hungry.

We lay in the sun watching the Sherpas and porters playing volleyball. Parvati, our sirdar Hem's nineteen-year-old sister joined us. A short walk later, we arrived at our campsite in the valley, and it was only two o'clock. The porters arrived one after the other and set up camp. We had our own tent. Hem's tent was on one side and the toilet, a small cone of canvas covering a hole and secured by two rocks, lay beyond. I sat reading, and a local girl approached with her friend. She showed me her face, which was covered with running sores and motioned for help. She was young and pretty. I called Hem over and he applied some ointment from his first-aid kit. This was their brutal world, with no medical help for even minor problems.

Evening arrived with dinner at seven, and we were called to the lantern glow of the dining tent. I could not believe that a table and four chairs had been carried over the passes on a porter's back for our comfort. Right after dinner I set up my sleeping bag on the hard ground in our tent and was asleep by 8:30. Dawn came all too soon, and the day's routine began again with tea served at the door of our tent. I would be "Mummy", and Gordie would be "Babu". Our sleepy faces appeared through the tent flap, and two "cook boys" squatted with electric smiles, a large kettle, and tin cups of steaming tea. This gave us time to collect our thoughts, dress, roll up our sleeping bags, and exit the tent so the porters could collapse and pack everything and get on their way. After a breakfast of toast, eggs, porridge, and more tea at a long table on the grass, we were on the trail. It was a 900 metre climb on endless stone steps to our lunch by a stream in the sunshine where I promptly fell asleep.

Starting off again was an effort when I was full of sleep and food, but my thoughts were of the porters carrying their weight on their backs. Their legs were as thin as sticks. We passed a three-year-old boy in rubber boots bearing his small backpack resolutely following his mother and I thought what softies we were. The next morning, I was sore from lying on the cold ground with only the thinnest of mats for comfort. Up and down we trekked until the stiffness disappeared, leaving bruises rubbing against my daypack. But then an old woman passed us, bent double with a load as large as she was. Her feet were bare. Porters carried their heavy loads in bare feet too through patches where snow had melted and turned to ice. How could I complain? A brassy Aussie girl in the shortest of shorts told us how much she knew about these mountains as she stopped to educate us. She was oblivious to the hostile glances local people tossed her way, hating to see such insensitivity to their conservative customs. The shy smile of a girl in the wooden tea shack at a bend in the trail provided us with a counterbalance. She had tea brewing on an open fire and generously offered us a cup. Three Swiss trekkers smoking grass at the top of the pass were busy enhancing their natural Himalayan high. Magnolia blossoms exploded on bare branches, and the sunlight shafted through the rhododendrons, creating orange halos around their trunks. We rested near the top of the pass, the Lamjura La, and were overwhelmed by the smell of feces. Garbage, paper, and used shoes lined the trail and what seemed to be hostile "you are rich, and I am poor" glances pierced us as we passed. The slopping sounds of bare feet sloshing through mud, the laughter of the Sherpas as they chattered, the blue of the sky, and the majesty of the mountains were all a jumble in our minds as we trudged on in silence. We had hot showers and apple pie at Junbesi, and I rubbed my bruised and raw hipbones. The cold seeped through to the sleeping bag again that night, and it was a relief to welcome dawn and an early start. We passed mani walls of prayers piled high with their stone tablets as we followed the contours of the juniper covered mountains. The mantra *Om Mani Padme Hum* – "Hail to the Jewel in the Heart of the Lotus" – was carved on each tablet as a devotional act. Always we moved to the left, the clockwise direction of the earth and universe, to release these prayers to the gods.

Everywhere, in harmony with the landscape, this Sanskrit mantra reminded us to be present. It was stamped on the many coloured scraps of cloth that fluttered in the wind. Flags atop wooden courtyard poles welcomed us with this message. It was carved into weathered rock faces; curled into old men's

Taksingdu La

prayer wheels as they twirled them, always clockwise, while warming their old bones in the sun on wooden benches. It was etched onto cylinders revolving in streams under their small wooden houses. With every breath, we inhaled these blessings.

After lunch by a river we climbed to a cheese factory above Ringmu, run by Mingma's aunt and uncle. They had learned the process from the Swiss, and made both goat and yak cheese. Mingma was our second Sherpa or guide. The Sherpas only carry their personal items in a daypack. They speak English in varying degrees and are paid more than the porters. Tibetan in origin, these tribes moved over the border to Nepal, settling in the Everest region six hundred years ago. "Sherpa" means "people of the East". Mingma's aunt was happy to see him, and served us tea by their fire. At fifty-four, she was already an old woman. In the next room in this sturdy stone house, a boy sat on the floor grinding corn by hand. Down the hill, two men sawed a log rhythmically, each at the end of the same long blade. Corn dried in the sun, and two puppies tumbled about in the yard nearby.

Above the settlement, we climbed to a pass called the Taksingdu La. Marked by a stone cairn, this pass separated the lower Solu district from the high Khumbu where Mount Everest reigns. On the other side was a steep descent through a surprisingly beautiful forest of magnolia blossoms and pink and red rhododendron flowers. But that night's campsite was in a grotty playground in Manidingmo, a filthy town with a disgusting toilet and ubiquitous dogs that barked all night long. My bruised hips filled my thoughts. Beauty, filth, and discomfort enhanced my compassion for the local people and focused my mind in a narrow beam on the now. "Be Here Now" had become my primary lesson.

The next morning, four women porters quit. The bags were too heavy. They were near their farm homes and did not want to continue into the high and colder country. Two more porters were hired,

THE SILENCE AND REMOTENESS
BROUGHT THOUGHTS OF THE
TIMELESSNESS OF EXISTENCE,
THE SHORTNESS OF LIFE AND
THE UNCERTAINTY OF DEATH
WHEN IT COMES.

and they smoked up before starting off. We crossed the terraces of the Kharikola, and for an hour and a half after lunch we trekked down, up, and along to our campsite. It was a perfect camp-spot overlooking two valleys and right below a Buddhist shrine called a stupa.

I climbed up to the stupa and passed by the wall of a small building. A wooden lintel marked the entrance to a small porch with two narrow wooden doors. I pushed, and they yielded to the pressure. The dim light inside revealed a giant drum suspended on one metal pin. The drum was covered with canvas on which were painted monsters, flowers, Buddhas, elephants, horses, sailboats, and rams' horns. It gave me the strangest feeling, alone in the semi-darkness, a frisson, as though something was about to be revealed through an undefined presence. Rope loops were nailed to the drum at the bottom. The entire cumbersome cylinder turned and one revolution caused a bell to ring. I could imagine the mind of an illiterate peasant absorbing two thousand years of teachings through these visual images, as it was in the Middle Ages.

Night fell, and across the valley the darkness was pierced here and there by the orange glow of tiny fires. The silence and remoteness brought thoughts of the timelessness of existence, the shortness of life, and the uncertainty of death when it comes.

In the morning, I awoke to the first light of day shining on the snow peaks. The stars were fading as dusky porters emerged from the open shed behind us. They shivered, clutching worn blankets to thin bodies and braced against the chill. Two men passed silently down the trail with empty woven baskets.

A rooster crowed and another day began – another day of magnolia and rhododendron blossoms and the smell of feces. Snotty-nosed kids with filth baked on by sun and smoke, washed and peed by the water pump. We were never alone. Along the trail, the Sherpas talked right behind me. One pounded the drum that accompanied us everywhere. My nerves were frayed. I longed to walk alone without Mingma one step behind. I had nothing to say to him, and that gulf between us bothered me as well. He continued on, pounding his drum.

> WE MET BOORS, LOUTS, DROP-OUTS, MISFITS, ATHLETES AND NOVELTY SEEKERS – ALL SEARCHING FOR A MEANING TO THEIR LIVES.

We arrived at a river below Lukla and met an obnoxious Scot in shorts, who had been running the trails, and thought we'd be impressed. A group of British soldiers showed up and cracked out beers. Loud laughter. We were close to other possible ways of experiencing travel in these mountains. Boors, louts, drop-outs, mystics, athletes, and novelty-seekers all seemed to be searching for a meaning to their lives. Nature could have the answer, or hardworking local people just being themselves as examples, or perhaps the exotic spiritual aura that seemed to permeate the landscape was the key. On a more practical level, steeling myself for being teased as a softie, I rented a foam mattress for

Tengboche Monastery

twenty cents and gave my bruised hips a softfoam treat.

Four days later at Tengboche Monastery, I was exploring the grounds, fully dressed with wool underwear, two sweaters, and a down jacket, trying to stay warm. It was mid-afternoon, and cold mist swirled around the yak pasture, raising the fine dust and coating everything in dirt. Our tents were pitched between mounds of yak dung. Above me, the monastery loomed, a strange medieval fortress-like structure. Monks chipped rocks, planed wood, and carried brush. The interior of the building was kept cold and dark by a heavy filthy curtain. Paintings and scraps of deteriorating cloth lined the walls. Buddhas, bowls of water, drums, and prayer wheels crowded the dim interior space. There was a patch of light at the top of steep stairs inside, where monks sat among the Buddhas and rags. Walls were varnished over and over again in an attempt to preserve what was left of the deteriorating paintings. The windows were covered with opaque white paper. The field in front of the monastery was jammed with trekkers, film crews, and expedition paraphernalia. A German tour group was having a lecture on the Gompa steps. As we left to climb higher, I watched some trekkers descending on our trail, and I half wanted to follow them down.

We continued up, however, now above 4,000 metres. I would be so happy to go up and come down in good health. This trek was graded as "very strenuous", whatever that meant. "Difficult," I think. And it was cold. I am the oldest woman Hem had ever guided up there. "How old are you, Mummy?" he inquired. I replied, "I'm only fifty-one, for heaven's sake." I thought back a few days to the climb from the awful yak pasture at Phakding and our delicious lunch on the rocks by the Duth Kosi in the warmth and sunshine.

The trail up to Namche Bazar was so steep and stony that I was frightened of taking a wrong step and pitching over the edge to instant death hundred of metres below. It was a relief to finally sight the village around the corner, but once again we spent two nights in the filth of a yak compound with the added indignity of slops being pitched out the window and down the wall of the building behind us. Dogs continued to bark all night here as well. The toilet was unbearably disgusting, and fine dirt coated everything, including our lungs.

In the midst of that ugliness, we went to a nearby "hotel" and sat in a third-floor room near a tailor who was stitching shoes, repairing backpacks, and humming quietly to himself. Two of the opaque paper window coverings were being replaced with glass. Outside, down the hill, a band of women hoed and planted potatoes, one digging, one throwing, and one covering in a timeless rhythm. The scene brought to mind the spring manuscript of the glorious medieval *Très Riches Heures du Duc du Berry*, a 15th-century book of hours painted in France, that illustrated the timeless change of seasons. In the spring manuscript, the artist showed the soft earth being plowed and seeded. The peasants wore tattered clothes then, and life was not idealized. Nor was it in my mind on that spare spring day.

We hiked up to the Everest View Hotel, a shell of a structure, rotting and empty. It was a Japanese hotelier's dream gone awry, too high for tourists and with too little oxygen available. Now it was slowly reverting to the Khumbu dust and rubble of the landscape. We passed Khumjung and the Hillary school with its oxygen bottle bell, and hiked over to Khunde Hospital where Canadian doctors struggled to be accepted by the community. People were reluctant to try western medicine. Some did not follow the directions carefully or accurately, and that gave them further proof that the medicine didn't work. In their minds, their medicine men or their monks were better sources of care.

I was almost getting used to dirt myself. Seven more days of walking and my clothes would stand alone stiff with the dirt. I had my birdbath in the morning and washed my hair in a glacial stream. These were small but wildly appreciated pleasures.
From Tengboche, we walked into a cool wind as if through a fairy tale. The ground was stonier and the peaks higher as we skirted the spectacular Mother's Jewelbox or Ama Dablam. To me this mountain was far more dramatic than Mount Everest.

Dingboche, at 4,350 metres, was higher than the tops of most peaks in Canada, and I had a headache from the altitude. I hoped it would go away. We had more climbing ahead, and we all felt lethargic.

The day before, I had my low depression day – in the snow by the world's highest monastery. There was no escape from the cold. How much longer until I could get out of there? Everyone huddled against the wind, while the porters crowded around a small fire. We dove into our sleeping bags at five in the afternoon. Dinner was a major event (again). The Coleman lantern provided some warmth in the dining tent, but it was minus two degrees Celsius and frost and a light dusting of snow covered the ground. We were beginning to talk of baths and luxuries like clean clothes.

We climbed to Lobuche at 4,940 metres and pitched our tents. Another headache throbbed behind my eyes, and I wondered if I could carry on. There was no way of knowing when serious altitude sickness would force me to descend, and I was apprehensive. I could die. Our guide was no help with his marginal English. As we trekked higher the pounding in my head intensified, my fingers began to swell like sausages, and my hands became numb. We had ascended too quickly, climbing in three days from

Tengboche, when the guidebook recommended a minimum of five. The company had shortened the number of nights. It was bitterly cold with nowhere to go to warm up. Another night fully dressed in a sleeping bag meant that when we woke up at 4:00 a.m. we were ready to go. In minus ten degrees, we ate breakfast by the feeble light of a lone candle.

By 4:30 a.m., prepared with a bag lunch and a flashlight, we began our climb. Two and a half hours to Gorak Shep and then on to Kala Pattar. I had no idea what lay ahead other than grim tales of death on the trail. The sky was studded with millions of stars. The Milky Way swept across the sky from north to south. Two shooting stars flared above the dark and menacing mountains. The air was as sharp and clear as glass crystal. Flutters of excitement competed with the ever-present pounding in my head. We started off in high spirits in the dark, walking for almost an hour along the edge of the mighty Khumbu glacier.

Slowly the giant moraine appeared in the dawn light. We were climbing through four-metre boulders, higher than ourselves, seemingly tossed there by Hercules from the domain of the gods above. Gordie had gone ahead with Hem and a fit young American girl. I was with Mingma and Lock, while Cyril plodded along behind. I gave in and let Mingma carry my pack. After a series of climbs and short descents, we arrived at a frozen lake and two huts. This was Gorak Shep, the most desolate spot in the world at 5,170 metres.

By now, the peaks were proclaiming their majesty in full sunlight against a deep ultramarine sky. It was a cloudless minus ten degrees. Above us loomed Kala Pattar, a steep climb culminating in a rocky peak at 5,554 metres. The first steep ascent took my breath away. I counted to 50 and rested on a rock. It was becoming increasingly difficult to breathe. Mingma stayed with me while Lock edged ahead.

At the top of this first climb the land sloped gently across a grassy meadow before the final enormous steep pitch. Even on the gradual slope I was moving more slowly. My legs felt weak and wobbly, rests were increasing, and I was beginning to gasp for air. The steepness was almost overwhelming – ten steps and then a five-minute rest. Ten more steps and I truly didn't think I could take one more. I felt sick.

The summit seemed no closer, my brain was confused, and I was giddy. Far below, Cyril sat on a rock. At least I was nearer to our goal. Finally, Mingma said, "Ten more minutes." After what seemed like hours later, I looked up to see Gordie wedging the flag of Canada into the rocks. I had to make it now after seventeen days. The goal was in view.

With all my strength, I pulled myself up among the massive boulders and collapsed by the flag. Pictures were taken. There was much delight and whooping. Not from me! I was barely conscious, directing a bleary gaze sideways at Everest and, down below me, at Everest base camp. Was I really at my goal? I staggered up to another site where someone took a photo of Gordie and me together with Mingma. "Please hurry," I moaned. "I absolutely have to descend!" Sick, giddy, and weak, I knew this pain would soon be over.

On our descent, Gordie and a Sherpa took a side trip to Base Camp. They were to meet us later that day at our Lobuche camp.

Kala Pattar with Pumori behind and Everest Base Camp below right.

We passed Cyril, who was still sitting on the same rock. He was so sick. I staggered by and continued down to Gorak Shep, where Mingma took me to a Sherpa teahouse. I collapsed on a mattress and fought nausea. A short time later, I joined Lock, Hem, Jetta, and Cyril near the long walk over the moraine. Hem and Jetta left us and carried on to Lobuche, leaving Mingma with the three of us. Lock lay on the ground, feeling sick, with Cyril beside him.

I felt a bit better. Lock and I lurched on ahead, taking ten steps and sitting, then twenty steps and collapsing on a rock. Slowly, we left Mingma with Cyril and our three packs.

We trudged ahead. Some people passed us on the way down and mentioned the sick man back there. The trail down stretched forever, and the hills of rocks were exhausting challenges. One man ran crazily towards us. "Get help," he shouted. "There's a very sick man back there." He saw that we were in poor shape ourselves and ran on to Lobuche.

Eventually Hem and Jetta ran towards us, filled with remorse for having abandoned Mingma to go for tea in Lobuche. By now, Mingma was carrying the 100-kilo Cyril on his back, and two American girls were carrying our packs. Lock and I stumbled into camp relieved, exhausted, and even hungry.

After an hour, Cyril appeared, swaying between the two Sherpas. Six men then gathered and carried him down to the medical clinic at Pheriche, where he was placed in a metal decompression tank. While I had accomplished my goal, I had come close to a serious and possibly fatal end. Finally, we could descend to warmer weather, showers, and clean clothes.

I awoke at midnight in Lobuche with a splitting headache and nausea. I was close to waking Hem to get me down the hill that night. I slept fitfully, and my breathing was ragged and difficult. None too soon, morning arrived, and we were finally able to leave this cold and hostile place. It was minus twelve degrees. With what seemed like giant steps as our lungs welcomed the denser air, we almost danced by the Khumbu glacier and climbed over the terminal moraine. Twenty stone piles a metre or so high, called chortens, faced across the valley towards Ama Dablam. These were memorials to the men who had died on Everest. We might have been among them on this ill-conceived journey.

> WE CLIMBED THROUGH BOULDERS HIGHER THAN OURSELVES, SEEMINGLY TOSSED THERE BY HERCULES FROM THE DOMAIN OF THE GODS ABOVE.

At Pheriche, we checked into the Himalayan Rescue Association to find out why we were so sick. The answer was chilling and simple. We had ascended far too quickly and had risked our lives. We should have taken five days instead of three. Cyril was lucky to feel better after spending the last 24 hours in a decompression chamber. Overweight and in his early fifties, he had suffered from acute pulmonary mountain sickness for several days. His problem had not been spotted by anyone and, too proud to reveal his pain, he had pressed on. This big mistake almost cost him his life. His lungs had filled with fluid, and he was to survive days of double vision on his return to Kathmandu.

The sun shone, and I felt elated and excited that this ordeal or adventure – depending on how you looked at it – was over, and I was alive. Warm weather beckoned. We climbed through the forest at Tengboche and burst into the monastery compound just minutes before Sir Edmund Hillary was expected. What a thrill it was to see him approach the stone gate with his Nepalese soldier aide. This had all happened by chance. We had no idea he would be coming to the monastery. The abbot was the first to greet him, and then the long line of monks all the way to the monastery steps waited to offer him a khata scarf blessing. By the time he arrived at the steps of the monastery, his head had almost disappeared under a cloud of white silk scarves.

It was a warm sunny day, and I sat on a point of land nearby looking 180 degrees over a silent, unspoiled world. I gazed at lammergeiers soaring in the updrafts. To be so in harmony with the universe is one of those rare feelings we all strive for, and this moment was special to me. We had walked 17 kilometres that day, and it had become warm enough to shed our wool tights and one sweater. But that night, despite my newfound comfort, I had vivid dreams involving fear.

Morning arrived with the usual bed tea and warm washing water. We started off down the mountain in high spirits. Oxygen flooded our lungs. At the bottom of the hill, near the Imje Khola, we splashed like children in the icy shallows of the river. Then it was uphill along the contour of the mountains with

Gord with Sir Edmund Hillary

Gravel landing strip at Lukla Airport

Ama Dablam always in our view.

We crossed a final ridge and descended through the dusty bowl where Namche Bazar was situated. Our dry and dusty yak compound was empty, but this was to be our tent spot for the night, and it was only noon. We ate lunch and Gordie, Lock, and I headed out to walk up and along a beautiful valley towards Thame, a village on the route to Tibet. Tiny iris plants revealed themselves along the trail, and we were back in pines and bare spring branches covered with pink blossoms. We were reluctant to return to the dust of Namche Bazar, where stony paths crisscrossed the bowl stripped bare of trees. We stopped for tea and apple pie at a corner of the main street and waited for dinner.

That night, we made the decision to walk all the way down to Lukla the following day, rather than travel for three hours to another grim yak compound. It was to be a seven and a half hour walk. Cyril's vision was still bad – he was seeing double.

We began our descent at seven the next morning in very high spirits. There is nothing like deep gulps of rich heavy air to improve your mood. The steep drop into the Dudh Kosi gorge was over in one hour, and we arrived at the Japanese Guest House in time for morning tea and a green salad. The owner grew his own vegetables. We fell upon the tender leaves and nothing could have tasted sweeter.

All afternoon, we passed green fields in the spring sun. A Japanese tour group, newly arrived from Lukla by air, fluttered by us. Their equipment was sparkling, and the women wore lipstick and shaded their heads under white umbrellas. We were such seasoned grubs by now that we eyed them as though they were aliens. They too glanced our way, but with aversion.

We tramped into Lukla by late afternoon. Hem beckoned us into a dark building around a corner and into an equally dark kitchen where a Sherpani tended a glowing fire. Wonder of wonders, a man was playing a guitar and singing Stevie Wonder and Bob Dylan songs. This could have been heaven. We ordered copious amounts of beer and many chocolate bars. Pasang appeared from nowhere with hot tea and cookies.

The gravel airstrip was beside our inn and at six o'clock the next morning we were at the departure building awaiting our flight. By eight-thirty a bell rang, which meant one plane had taken off from Kathmandu. It was hazy, and no instrument flying was allowed at this airstrip. Would our plane be able to land? This was always the way at Lukla. Sometimes it took days to get out. There were many people hoping to leave, and as flights landed all morning, the weather could deteriorate. We were on the last flight before noon.

Fortunately for us we heard a roar thirty minutes later, and a small plane bumped up the gravel airstrip and ground to a halt, stirring up a tornado of dust so we knew they were flying. No one seemed to know what planes would land as the clouds increased over the course of the morning. By 11:00 a.m., we were told that our flight had taken off from Kathmandu. The STOL aircraft landed at Lukla and after the pilot finished his tea, we climbed aboard with great relief.

The takeoff was downhill, and the runway was bumpy. The engine revved to a high pitch, the pilot released the brake, and suddenly we jerked ahead and wobbled into the air. A mountain directly in front of us veered by my window as the plane banked sharply, and we rose into the clouds. As I remembered that Hillary's wife and son had lost their lives in a similar plane at the Kathmandu airport, I took faint solace in the thought that our pilot had done this trip many times.

It was only a three-quarter hour trip to Kathmandu. We landed in haze without mishap, and all of us applauded the pilot. We were safely back where we had begun. For two days, we bathed in warm water and devoured the buffets at the hotel, eating everything forbidden by the traveller's mantra "cook it, peel it, or forget it" – lettuce, ice cream, tomatoes, and beefsteak. The predictable result, of course, was to endure the "Kathmandu two-step" a euphemism for diarrhea. It was almost worth it.

Bags stuffed with souvenirs, we flew to Hong Kong and then home to our new world in Vancouver. Our lives had changed dramatically. While setting down roots in a large metropolis, we both harboured the idea of developing an adventure travel business.

It wasn't long before a return visit to Nepal became a serious discussion. The constant pull of the Himalayas led to Gord signing up with an Australian expedition to the Annapurnas in the fall of 1988. This was to be a father / daughter experience. Gord, age 56 and Erin age 20, would trek to Copra Ridge on the west shoulder of Annapurna South to test the possibility of taking clients to this area.

What followed was the creation of Everest Trekking Canada.

Ama Dablam, Khumbu 6,812 metres

chapter 2

THE ANNAPURNA CIRCUIT
TRANSFORMING MOMENTS

1989 | GAIL

A five-hour bone-jarring bus trip on a pot-holed road west from Kathmandu took us to a dusty truck exchange. We switched from the relative comfort of the bus to an open army truck and rattled up a dirt road for another three hours. Along the way to meet our trekking crew we traversed shallow streams and laboured up almost vertical hillsides. One of our group asked whether the cancellation insurance for this trip meant he could apply for it on the spot.

Disgorged from the truck, our bedraggled bunch blinked into the hot afternoon sun and pondered the path at the trailhead. I had a bad cough and others had diarrhea. There was no choice but to begin walking. A Sherpa carried my pack after finding me head-in-hands by the path. He gave me an umbrella as shade from the sun and told me to walk slowly. On arrival at our first campsite I only wanted to sleep, so I skipped dinner and tucked myself into my tent. The porters were happy to have our dining tent to sleep in when everyone retired early.

The Annapurna Circuit is one of the world's most demanding treks. For twenty-one days, we would travel on foot more than 200 kilometres. Our goal was to climb over the Thorung La, a 5,400 metre pass, and walk down the other side in a wide U-shape around the Annapurna massif where mountains rise to 8,000 metres in height.

It was November and the poinsettias were in bloom. At Bahundanda we stopped briefly under a tree and soon were surrounded by villagers and begging children. The local people had such relaxed expressions on their faces compared to the tight-lipped trekkers we met. The trekkers projected an aura of arrogance and seemed to feel that they were more worthy if they were travelling independently, or if they were younger than we were, or if they carried mountain-climbing equipment. They were not a friendly lot. Many were shocked at the number of westerners they encountered, more than 200 a day, when they were expecting to be among the pioneers of this unique way of being and travelling.

We passed the village of Tal in the rain and were delighted to find that we would be staying in a lodge. Climbing to the third floor, we were shown a small room separated from the next one with slats of wood. Each room had a basic lock, a wooden bed, two nails in the wall, and a very thin, very dirty foam mattress. It looked great to us! I was shivering with cold and by now the rain was coming down in sheets. Soon it was dark, but we could still hear the village children playing outside in the mud.

This was our first adventure with Tashi Sherpa and our young trail cook, Maila. We were to have chicken that night. Sange, our assistant cook, had been carrying three live ones in his pack all day. I could hear their squawks as their necks were snapped, and they were disembowelled. This reality was far from the wrapped breasts and thighs on local grocery shelves at home. These birds were tough from running up and down the mountains, but it was a luxury to have meat.

Morning came all too soon as dogs, chickens, clanging pots and pans, and throat clearings made sleep impossible. I talked to the local doctor who handled minor health problems such as worms, scabies, and conjunctivitis, but anyone really sick had to lie down at home or in a hotel near the clinic. A few basic medicines were all he had. We probably had more choices in our first aid kit.

We trekked past Dharapani, a Tibetan village, and noticed a change in the people. They were cleaner, and the women wore turquoise and coral. This was Buddhist country. At Ratamron we came to a hot spring and threw off our clothes to splash about in a shallow rocky groove despite the cold. The opportunity to be clean from head to toe was rare while trekking; bathing was usually accomplished in a shallow tin bowl in the morning and evening.

It was minus two degrees in the morning, and for the first time, we put on our woolly underwear. We were almost above tree line and beginning to walk ever higher into snow. From that day on, every morning would be below freezing until we were well beyond the pass.

Trekkers streamed onto the trail above Pisang. As this was one of the most popular treks in Nepal, the trail was crowded. At Manang, 3,540 metres, we rested for two days, enjoying a lodge and its rudimentary showers. Vultures soared over the roof, rising on gentle updrafts. Children playing below disappeared in and out of the smoke of the cooking fires. The sun was hot on our arms, and I felt connected to a timeless sense of peace.

We would think of this pleasant interlude as we climbed 1,800 metres over the next two days. The following afternoon, after an all-day uphill climb, we reached the lodge at Thorung Phedi. The rooms were crowded, hot, noisy, and as charming as mini-storage. Our fellow trekkers came from France, Israel, Australia, Germany, and Italy, and our common bond was the suffocating atmosphere of palpable tension, anticipation, and nervous energy. We would all soon face the challenge of the Thorung La.

At one o'clock the next morning, most of us were awake, and everyone was up and dressed by three. It was minus ten degrees. This was the last shelter before the pass 1,000 metres above us.

Headlamps moving through the darkness dotted the trail. These were the trekkers trudging up like the

miners in Snow White. With increasingly laboured breathing, I too toiled upward in ever thinning air. My heart felt taxed to the limit, my legs cramped with lactic acid, and I felt dizzy. I desperately wanted to lie down. Aware of the physical and mental challenges, I knew I never wanted to do something like this again. Never! What was I doing here? I gasped for air. Surely the top was near, but as one hill curved into the next, there was always another hill to climb.

Gordie fed me chocolate. His strength and resolve were impressive. The stars began to fade one constellation after the next – the Pleiades, Orion's Belt, and finally, one by one, those of the upside-down Dipper.

Coloured jackets appeared in the distance. The wind was strengthening and the temperature dropping. We had to be at the pass before very strong winds developed. Suddenly, Gordie appeared, waiting to greet me and climb the last 100 metres to stand in sunshine on the Thorung La at 5,416 metres. We had arrived! One of our trekkers had rented a horse to take her up to the pass. Another commented that getting to the top, a three-hour dark uphill slog in thin air, was tougher than running a marathon.

Tashi had a satellite phone but no advanced weather reports. We were aware of our vulnerability to a change in the weather conditions, and it was reassuring to have him guide us through the moonscape surroundings. In hindsight, we would not have survived a serious storm. Good fortune was on our side, and our crossing was a success. As it was too cold to linger, we joined others to descend to Muktinath, 1,800 metres below.

At our village campsite, we celebrated our accomplishment. Muktinath means "the place of salvation" where Guru Rinpoche stopped on his way to deliver Buddhism to Tibet. We were saved from all kinds

Mani wall at Manang

of dangers – storms, altitude sickness, and bone weariness. Sitting in the late afternoon sun with Dhaulagiri in the distance, we drank beer and ate a yak dish called soukouti, a meat dish salted and fried in garlic. It was like heaven, but with our increasing experiences of yin and yang, we were to pay for our celebration by being up all night with diarrhea. How many times do the Himalaya have to teach us these simple facts?

Walking down past Jharkot was a day that could only be described as ethereal. Oxygen flooded our lungs, bringing an exhilarating sense that something deep and life-changing was being revealed. The ultramarine sky, thin sparkling air, and silence broken only by the chanting of a farmer far below, were impressions to cherish and cling to. The farmer followed his two oxen and wooden plow, turning over the earth for the last time before winter. He, his animals, the plow and furrow, the ochre and olive of the rocks and symphony of browns in the valley seemed in harmony with the heavens. We were all one.

Gazing back and up, we could only marvel at where we were and whence we had come. Such peaceful sights were interrupted when we noticed an old farmer slowly walking towards us. He begged for any medicine we might be able to give to him. Our sirdar held both his hands, looked into his eyes with deep compassion. He admitted that there was no way we could help him. The farmer passed by slowly and reluctantly, ascending to his hut. Sick and dying, he would need treatment far beyond the rudimentary medicine we carried in our first aid kit.

That night we camped in Kagbeni, a fortified village at the junction of two rivers: the mighty Kali Gandaki and the Thak Kola, both rising in Tibet. We ate our dinner upstairs by firelight in a local house. Dusky faces surrounded us. Tucked into a corner of the room, a baby nursed at her mother's breast, and then slept to the murmuring music of Nepali voices. A child revealed an ammonite stone containing an ocean mollusk fossil from 140 million years ago, before India slid under the Asian continent causing the formation of the Himalaya. We walked on the Kali Gandaki's stony plain through fine dust and wind, past the apple orchard village of Marpha and on to the forested town of Kalopani, where we camped in a wild marijuana field. It was a race to the "See You Lodge" and buckets of warm water for washing. Kalopani was where the river descended 1,500 metres through the river gorge and down to the village of Tatopani. There were many suspension bridges on this part of the trail in various states of disrepair.

A curious event had occurred in March prior to our trek departure back in Vancouver. Our niece Martha had been scheduled to see Rosalind Hein, a psychic living in Vancouver. At the last moment, she had to cancel, so Gordie filled in for her. At the given time, he knocked on the back door of a house in our Vancouver neighbourhood. Rosalind came to the door and said, "I was expecting Martha."

"Well, you've got Gord," he replied.

He was invited to sit at her kitchen table, whereupon she began to review his life story. She told him that he was starting a new business involving the leadership of groups in mountainous areas and that a tall woman with dark hair would have a very difficult time crossing a bridge on our first trek. She assured him that he would successfully manage the situation, and all would remain safe. He felt shivers down his spine.

Trekking to Thorung Phedi

Two weeks before this meeting, Gwendda, a tall woman with dark hair, had been in Vancouver to discuss the trek. She had only one reservation – the crossing of swinging bridges. In spite of her fears she was keen to go.

So six months later, there we were, crisscrossing the Kali Gandaki gorge on swinging bridges on our way to Tatopani. Gordie couldn't get Rosalind's prediction out of his mind. He stayed with Gwendda for the first day, and she proved to be unconcerned. With fears allayed, he put any uneasiness about bridges out of his head and settled in to enjoy the adventure.

Late one afternoon we rounded a corner of the trail to find below us a wooden bridge under repair. The 10-metre span was gone, and villagers were preparing a temporary crossing using hand-hewn timbers. There were no handrails. We stopped where the trail ended at the rushing river and gaped at the chasm before us. Gwendda was stunned when she absorbed the scene, and slumped to the ground.

In Gordie's mind, he heard Rosalind's words: "You will organize a successful crossing, and all members of the group will be safe."

We gathered at the edge of the gorge and assessed the crossing on the loose, uneven timbers. The Kali Gandaki waters roiled fifteen metres below us. It was a difficult moment for everyone, particularly Gwendda. Finally, each trekker had accomplished the terrifying crossing, one by one, being led with both hands on a Sherpa's shoulders.

Gwendda, who could not watch, was the last to cross. Helping her up, Gordie told her to place her hands on the Sherpa's shoulders and to look directly at the back of his neck. With another Sherpa behind, the three crossed the unstable timbers. We held our collective breath and exhaled with relief when she reached us. Gordie never returned to see Rosalind to tell her the bridge story.

This had been a long trek and much too challenging for most of our untested trekkers. One woman developed a stress fracture in her right foot and walked for more than a week in pain. A noticeable weariness spread through the group in the last week. Everyone lost weight. In spite of these difficulties, we concluded the trek with a universal feeling of accomplishment and camaraderie.

Like any great adventure, there are moments of white fear, but the hope is to experience the most rare of life-transforming moments. Interesting things don't happen simply by brushing your teeth and slipping into a cozy bed at home. We had set the bar high with our choice of the 21-day Annapurna Circuit for our first commercial trek. It was a learning experience that became the template for Everest Trekking travels in the future.

On Tashi's recommendation, we included customized duffle bags in the trek fee. These sturdy bags were designed to hold a maximum weight of 15 kilograms. Green was the chosen colour with the company name and website address printed on both sides. This way they were easy to spot and count in airports. As the standard load for a porter was two duffle bags, having bags of equal size and shape simplified the morning division of loads by the sirdar.

We found from this experience that two weeks on the trail was the preferred length of time, and ten clients was the most efficient number. If we were to do longer treks in the high country we would need to be carefully selective of the group make-up.

We learned to include staff gratuities in the land price, along with key luxuries such as flying to the head of the trail, using a lodge at the conclusion of a trek, and hosting a high-end Nepali farewell dinner in Kathmandu.

Because this trip was successful in so many ways, we knew we would take more tours using a similar format. Tashi was our dream partner, organizing all the details once we landed in Nepal, and we were keen to return home and spread the word about this beautiful land and its people. Everest Trekking Canada was launched, and we were on our way to exciting times.

The bridge over the Kali Gandaki

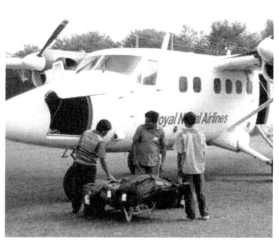

de Havilland Twin Otter

chapter 3

SHERPA FRIENDS OF NAMCHE BAZAR

GORD

THE FAMILY

Our partner Tashi Sherpa's engineering studies at Tribhuvan University preceded his opportunity to train as a mountaineering guide in the French Alps. He was one of the first Nepalis to graduate from the École Nationale de Ski et d'Alpinisme in Chamonix. He remained in Europe for two years while he honed his skills, climbing extensively in the Alps and instructing in Norway. Fellow mountaineers with whom he became friends included Sir Edmund Hillary, Maurice Herzog, and Reinhold Messner, as well as Hans Kammerlander, renowned for his ski descents of Everest and Nanga Parbat.

While teaching and guiding at a mountaineering school in the Annapurna region at Manang, Tashi made the first ascent of Bhrikuti Peak.

In 1988, the climbing associations of Nepal, China, and Japan organized a tri-national climb of Mount Everest funded by the Chinese and Japanese governments. Tashi was chosen to lead the Nepalese team climbing from the Tibet side. It was a highly publicized event with the first on-site television coverage. For reasons unknown, all climbers were ordered by the Chinese organizers to cut their attempts short and descend. The Nepal team was within a hundred metres of the summit at the time. They had no choice but to retrace their steps.

In 1985, two young Canadian girls walked into the Everest Trekking office looking for a trekking guide. Nancy Morison and her friend had been working in Japan and had come to Nepal for a mountain holiday. Tashi happened to be available, and the rest is history. He and Nancy married five years later in 1990.

I attended their wedding in Kathmandu that November. The reception, following a private Buddhist ceremony, was held in the garden of the Hotel Shangri-La. I was honoured to escort the bride into the garden to be greeted by 400 guests. Sherpa men wore the traditional long black robes and brown felt fedoras with the brims turned up. The Sherpa women were resplendent in their formal long dresses and multi-colored aprons. Businessmen sported dark suits with black topi hats, and the Nepali women wore saris. A small musical group played in one corner of the garden. Staff served exotic drinks from trays. Food tables were everywhere. The evening concluded with guests offering khata scarves and gifts to the bride and groom. Tashi and Nancy sat while hundreds of scarves covered their shoulders in layers of silky fabric.

At the time of their marriage Nancy spoke French and Japanese, as well as English. Within a year, she was able to speak Nepali and a little of the Sherpa dialect. On her mother's next visit to Nepal, she was proud to be able to translate a conversation between Carol and Tashi's mother Phurdiki.

Over our 25-year partnership we have brought 76 groups, more than 700 clients, to Nepal and into the caring hands of Tashi and Nancy. Our most popular destinations have been the Khumbu, Annapurna, Solu and Gorkha. Tashi and Nancy performed background heroics, dealing capably with bureaucracy, unreliable transport services, weather contingencies, holiday closures, and unexpected strikes. When one arrangement failed, we always knew they would be working to find an alternate solution.

Tashi and Nancy are the parents of Jimmy, born in 1991, and Tenzing, born in 1994. Nancy and the boys moved to Vancouver in 2005.

Tashi is currently executive director of the Himalayan Trust, an organization that provides funds

Nancy and Jimmy   *Ang Pasang*   *Phurdiki*

to help the people of the Nepal Himalaya realize their educational, health, economic, and cultural aspirations. The Trust was founded and led by Sir Edmund Hillary from 1960 until his death in 2008. The office of the Trust is located in Kathmandu.

Phurdiki, Tashi's mother, was born in 1935 (the year of the pig) in Namche Bazar, Khumbu. The origins of the village date back 500 years to a time when the Sherpas emigrated from Tibet. Phurdiki's family could be referred to as "old establishment" in the Khumbu. The population of Namche at the time of her birth was about 500 souls (all with the family name of Sherpa). There was little, if any, contact with the outside world. Education and medical services were limited, and Kathmandu was ten days away by foot and horse. Life was not easy in this remote hillside settlement.

She and her three brothers grew up with no electricity or running water. There was no hospital, dental clinic, or organized school. Namche Bazar's water flowed from a spring at the base of the village. Each morning the first chore for the children was to carry water up to the house in containers that weighed from ten to fifteen kilograms. The common source of heat was wood cut from the forests in valleys below. It wasn't until 1992 that power came to the village from an Austrian-built hydro plant at Thame, a two-hour walk away. Shortly thereafter water pumps were installed and by the following year running water was available to all residents. Glass was beginning to replace paper for windows as well.

Phurdiki came from a line of traders who made an annual trek over the Nangpa Pass (5,700 metres) to Tingre in Tibet. She married Ang Pasang of Khumjung, and they settled in Namche Bazar to raise their four children: Tashi (1957), Dorjee (1959), Nima (1962) and Ang Kenji (1968). She and her husband traded dzopkyos (yak/cow crossbreed) for wool and precious stones. The children walked uphill for an hour to attend the Sir Edmund Hillary School in Khumjung. Hillary was keen to give back to the Sherpa community for all their help and, as one of the many ways he expressed his love and admiration, he built this school for the area's children. The school bell was an empty metal oxygen tank and hung from a pillar near the front door.

Kenji remembers the annual departure of her parents to trade in Tibet. "It would be at night with no advanced notice to villagers. The Lama would be secretly consulted about an auspicious date. All preparations would be performed quietly, and at the appointed hour the caravan of more than forty yaks would rumble out of town to be gone for six to eight weeks." In 1962, with the date set to leave for Tibet, there was no question of Phurdiki staying behind to give birth to her third son. Nima was born in a tent on the Tibetan plain.

The dzopkyos were purchased on credit in the Solu district, a fertile valley four days' walk below Namche Bazar. The herd of 60 to 80 head would plod over the Nangpa La to the Tibet plain. Leading the animal train would be Phurdiki, the trail boss. Ang Pasang took up the rear. The animals were traded for sheep's wool, which was then sold in Kathmandu. The transaction would finally be completed with payment to the Solu owner later in the year. The net proceeds would be used to purchase goods from south Nepal and India for resale in Namche Bazar.

The first two-storey house in Namche Bazar, known as Khangba Thenga, belonged to Phurdiki's parents. She inherited this medieval dwelling and raised her four children there. We visited many times. The ground floor was used as shelter for the animals, and they provided necessary heat for the living quarters upstairs. The Gompa, located in the largest room, was a miniature monastery containing a bookshelf for the traditional 108 Buddhist prayer books and an altar to the Buddha and other deities. Benches for sleeping lay along two of the walls. The next most important room was the kitchen. Copper pots gleamed on shelves, and an open fire burned in a clay oven. The sweet perfume of potato pancakes and rice would percolate through the rooms. Chhang bubbled and fermented in brass-strapped wooden containers. Phurdiki offered us this rice beer from the moment we arrived until we reluctantly had to leave.

Phurdiki and Ang Pasang's travels taught them the importance of an education for their children. Each child made the 400 metre daily climb over the mountain to the Sir Edmund Hillary public school at Khumjung before being sent to a private school in Kathmandu.

Today, Tashi is an engineer who speaks seven languages. He lives in Kathmandu and has recently completed construction of a modern trekker's lodge at Lobuche.

THE WEDDING OF KALDEN AND KENJI

Kalden and Ang Kenji Sherpa, who now live and work in Vancouver, were married in 1996 in a traditional Sherpa wedding at her family home in Namche Bazar. This astrologically auspicious day, chosen specifically by the Lama of Tengboche, brought together the family of Kalden Sherpa from Solung in the Solu district and the family of Ang Kenji Sherpa of Namche Bazar. The villages are five mountainous walking days apart.

The wedding day began on a clear crisp morning, as the sun rose from behind Thamserku peak and flooded the village with enough warmth to melt the frost on the village roofs. At mid-day, the sound of helicopter rotors echoed from the valley below. Kalden, the groom, and his Sherpa family were arriving in 21st-century style at the Namche Bazar helipad. Dressed in full Sherpa wedding regalia, the family descended on a trail that traversed the steep face of the mountain above the village. Leading the procession was the village Lama, carrying an urn of burning juniper to cleanse the path. This same Lama was an "ice doctor", setting the ladders in the Khumbu icefall for the Everest climbers each spring and fall, a dangerous job that pays well.

It was a splendid sight, with the groom dressed in a full-length yellow brocade robe topped with a circular hat in vibrant red and orange. He resembled a storybook potentate. Sherpa wedding clothes and jewellery are outstanding. The men wore long black cloaks, high leather boots, and fedoras with the brim turned up on one side. The women dressed in colourfully embroidered dresses. Lavish necklaces of dzi stones and gold and silver boxes were encrusted with turquoise, coral, and pearls.

The women in Kenji's family greeted the procession in their embroidered otter-lined hats. Prayer flags flapped along the ridgeline of the house, and the scent of burning juniper permeated the air at the start of this ancient Sherpa ceremony.

A Buddhist wedding does not feature the bride and groom as in Western cultures. Instead, it is the coming together of two families through a series of ceremonies spread over a number of months. Following an agreement between the families, the Lama of the groom's family formally asks permission from the bride's family for the couple to marry.

To open the ceremony, the Lama welcomed everyone in a speech that praised the qualities of those in the room. I couldn't understand his words but, judging by the gales of laughter and rejoinders that came from the audience, his speech must have been witty and light-hearted. He gave a Tibetan blessing for the house, the food, and the families, read the bride's dowry (land, carpets, jewellery), and joined the bride and groom in marriage. The bride pledged her allegiance to her husband's family. It was a highly emotional moment for everyone and both joyful and sad for the bride as she presented gifts to each member of her family. She was leaving for Canada, a foreign land far from those she loved.

The host family ensured that the guests' glasses were constantly topped up throughout the day with tea, chhang, the potent mountain beer, or scotch served from three-litre bottles. Juniper branches continued to be burned in the courtyard as a ritual cleansing with smoke rising to mingle with the fluttering prayer flags.

The service was followed by dinner and dancing. Sherpa dancing is performed in a line. Three or more men or women link arms, and through a series of complicated steps, they move back and forth to music while someone chants. Later, everyone danced to the traditional music of a large stringed instrument, while the host circled the room filling glasses and encouraging laggards to drink up with a "che, che, che."

The echoes of the wedding party revelry rang through the village well into the night only to be repeated for the next two days. Sherpas are a hardy people, and they demonstrated stamina throughout the long and extravagant party. Recognizing my inability to keep up with my comrades, I slipped outside to enjoy the moonlight bathing the snow-capped peaks above the village.

It was a halcyon moment for the entire area, the family, and the wedded couple.

Kalden and Kenji returned to Vancouver to start their life together. Kalden joined Aquabus, a company that operated ferry boats in False Creek. He became known as the only Sherpa ship captain in North America. Kenji graduated as a licensed practical nurse. They bought a house in east Vancouver. Their two children, Dechen and Yonden, have been enrolled at Shawnigan Lake School and the University of Victoria respectively.

Phurdiki, Kenji's mother, died in 2003 and Ang Pasang, her father, died in Kathmandu in 2015. Both Dorjee and Nima, Kenji's other brothers, are married with children and live in Namche Bazar, where they operate two bakeries, a money exchange, a water-bottling plant, a guesthouse and hotel. Although Kenji and Kalden live far from their families, they visit Nepal regularly.

The wedding Lama

chapter 4

LEADERSHIP CHALLENGED

1991 | GORD

Following a near-perfect trek to Copra Ridge in the fall of 1990, it was time to spread our wings and return to the Khumbu with our third ETC trekking group. We had this image of perfection in mind, hoping for great weather, wonderful food, and a compatible group.

Because trekking in high country can challenge people up to and even sometimes beyond their mental and physical limits, they must dig deep to deal with what they are able to achieve. Some fare better than others. This trip to the Khumbu was to push the limits on all fronts and test my leadership skills.

Our 45-minute Twin Otter flight from Kathmandu landed on the gravel strip at Phaplu in the Sherpa district of Solu. The first three days began with a bang. Spring weather in the Himalaya can be unsettled with showers and thunderstorms. Camping on the third day, high above the Tubten Choling Monastery on an exposed ridge, we were hit with a powerful electrical storm that brought high winds and heavy rain. Most trekkers were deep in their sleeping bags while the Sherpas busily dug drainage trenches around the tents and double-tied the ropes as the storm approached. One trekker recalls telling her terrified tent mate to count the seconds between the flash and the thunder so she would know how close the storm was. Gail put on her glasses so she would see where she was going if we were blown away. In the morning, we assessed the damages – everyone was accounted for but the charpi (toilet tent) had disappeared down the valley, and the cook tent had collapsed. Otherwise, we were all in one piece.

As a reward for braving the wild night, Rinzi Sherpa, our sirdar, led us down the mountain to the village of Ringmu and to his nearby farm for the night. The 13 trekkers hung up wet clothes and spread their sleeping bags on every available metre of floor. Jiri Maila prepared a feast for us in Rinzi's kitchen, which included Mustang coffee for an after-dinner drink – two parts coffee and one part each of honey and rum – that floated us right into our sleeping bags.

The next day we crossed the Taksingdu La and entered the Khumbu district, descending 1,300 metres to the Dudh Kosi. From there it was a five-day trek up to Namche, the amazing bazaar in the sky and home to the Sherpa culture for 500 years. Close by were the towering peaks of Ama Dablam, Thamserku, and the Everest group. We had entered the throne room of the mountain gods.

Tony, who came with climbing credentials, approached me at lunch on the second day to complain that there was no hot water for him to wash his socks. He pouted when I pointed to the stream as a possibility or suggested he wait till evening when hot water would be available. He had difficulty with the daily routine of the trek, and by our fourth evening in camp, he remained in his tent at dinnertime. By this time, I had lost my patience and asked a fellow trekker, known as TJ, to persuade him to come to dinner.

TJ to Tony through the tent fabric: "Come on out for dinner. Maila has cooked a fresh chicken." Tony in a muffled voice: "Mumble mumble – I'm not coming."

Later, when a special dessert was brought to the table, I asked TJ to try again. TJ: "C'mon – come to the table. Maila has baked an apple pie!"

Tony to TJ: "Mumble mumble – get lost."

Finally, after six days, I asked Tony if he would prefer to return to Kathmandu and catch an early flight home. For the first time in a week a smile of relief crossed his face. He thanked me, promptly packed his bag, and with a Sherpa guide departed camp to find his way home to Canada. Before leaving, he generously donated his new red down jacket to a small porter with a cleft lip. The porter wore it proudly for the remainder of the trip.

John, a friend from Winnipeg, was part of our group. John grew up in Holland and later moved to Winnipeg, two areas with flat terrain. A mutual friend and soon-to-be trek leader, Gary, who was part of our first organized trek in 1989, had sparked John's enthusiasm for a Himalayan adventure. Early in the trek, we were faced with the Dudh Kosi valley and a trail that skirted precipices and crossed steep and scary pitches with excessive exposure. John quickly discovered that he suffered from acrophobia, an irrational but very real fear of heights. To help him, Rinzi Sherpa walked beside him for the remainder of the trek and held his arm as needed.

Above Lukla, the river gorge narrowed, and several swinging bridges crisscrossed the rushing torrent. Most of the bridges were shaky wooden cantilevered spans with low railings. Some of the walkways had rotten boards with rock-filled holes and tattered prayer flags tied to the railings to ward off evil spirits. They were not designed to humour those suffering from acrophobia.

John had brought his father's walking stick, a family heirloom from pre-war days in the Alps. It was decorated with small metal plates of famous Swiss mountain resorts visited in bygone years. As we approached a particularly rickety cable bridge, I went ahead to make sure it was clear before John and Rinzi climbed the platform to begin the crossing. As soon it was empty of trekkers and animals, I signalled to them to proceed, not knowing that a fully loaded yak was about to enter from the opposite side. As John and Rinzi inched their way across the narrow and unstable bridge, I was horrified to see the yak and his enormous load begin his crossing from the other side. As Rinzi and John gingerly turned on the bridge to retrace their steps, his walking stick was jarred loose from his backpack and fell into the turbulent water.

A few days later John became noticeably weaker and realized he could not continue. He reluctantly stayed behind in Namche Bazar and waited to rejoin the group on our descent.

Following our acclimatization day in Namche Bazar, and now missing two of our trekkers, we climbed higher to the Tengboche Monastery, where we visited the Rinpoche for a blessing. We needed this, because the next day we were to have another bridge incident.

At the start of our treks we discuss the danger of river crossings in Nepal. Steep embankments, fast-moving water, and beautiful surroundings offer perfect settings for photographs. However, with the eye composing through the camera lens, the mind forgets the danger in moving near a steep drop. Paying more attention to a perfect setting than to personal safety can result in a tragic accident. We had been part of the recovery of a body from another trek group the previous year in the Annapurna region, and we did not want a repeat occurrence.

An hour above the monastery, the trail crossed the Dudh Kosi. Far below, the rushing torrent tumbled through a narrow opening in the rocks. From the bridge, one had a spectacular view of Ama Dablam.

Tashi and I were following the group on a particularly sunny morning, and as we came into view of the bridge we could see TJ preparing to take a photo of Ama Dablam from the edge of the gorge. He had crossed the bridge, looked up to the mountain, and found the perfect spot. Stepping off the trail, he inched his way down the steep embankment to frame the view. Camera to his face, he was oblivious of the danger of falling into the gorge.

Before I could shout an alarm, Tashi held my arm and said, "Don't call – you will distract him. Pray to whatever god you wish for his safety." Holding our breath, we watched as TJ calmly took his photo, stepped away, and climbed back up to the trail. We had all dodged a bullet that day!

It is always a relief to descend to the warmth of the Kathmandu valley and the hot showers and the comfortable beds of the Kathmandu Guest House. We traditionally celebrate the conclusion of our trips with a grand final dinner at a Nepali restaurant. I decided that we needed to recognize each trekker with a small token of Nepal. Gail and I assembled a variety of Nepali memorabilia, but I was stuck when it came to John. He needed something special. A Nepali walking stick for him would have been ideal but none could be found. Passing a secondhand shop, I spotted a tray of military medals. Eureka! After rummaging through a surprising array of medals, I asked the clerk for the award for highest bravery, and there it was. Mounted on a bronze star of Nepal was a tiny porcelain national flag. This was a fitting gift for this brave trekker.

Following dinner there were many impromptu speeches, and I gave out the small mementos of Nepal to each person. John was last to step forward. He was dressed in full Nepali regalia. I spoke of John's bravery despite his vertigo, his constant good humour, and the admiration the group felt for him. As I pinned the medal on his lapel, tears came to his eyes. He spoke of his love of the country and his affection for the people he had met. There was not a dry eye in the room. A few months after our return to Canada, the phone rang in the ETC office. It was John calling from Winnipeg: "Gord, when can I return to Nepal with you? I would so love to be with those people again in that amazing country!" While he had the will to return, he came to realize that his body wasn't up to the challenge, and the lure of the high mountains had to become a cherished memory.

This was not the perfection I was hoping for with near-miss accidents, tumultuous weather, and challenges among the clients. Limits were tested, and I learned about leading people through difficult conditions. At the final dinner, I realized that I had accomplished my goal to provide a life-enhancing adventure, and I was motivated to continue.

Kathmandu Guest House Garden

chapter 5

LOST ON ANNAPURNA

1992 | GORD

Our group of eight hardy trekkers left Kathmandu bound for the west shoulder of Annapurna South and Kare Tal–at 4,500 metres, one of the three sacred lakes in Nepal. Each year, thousands of devout Hindu and Buddhist pilgrims climb through the barren landscape at the August full moon to perform puja (prayers) by the tiny lakeside shrine. We planned to follow these footsteps in unusually perfect fall weather. We were repeating a trek I had done twice before, first in 1988 with our daughter Erin and a group from Australia, and again in the spring of 1990 with a large group from Vancouver. This was to be Everest Trekking's fifth organized trek in Nepal.

The Copra Ridge trek is rated as strenuous. Over the first six days the route climbs 3,000 metres to reach an exposed ridge looking down into the Kali Gandaki gorge, three times the depth of the Grand Canyon. Across the void rises Dhaulagiri, the world's sixth highest mountain. Above the campsite, the peaks of Nilgiri, Annapurna l, and Annapurna South form a majestic panorama.

Lynn joined our group in Kathmandu. She had been teaching school there at the time and had trekked with us the previous year in the Langtang area. She decided to join us, but not as a client, and as she was a strong trekker who had completed a number of solo routes in Nepal, she was a wonderful addition to the group.

There are many advantages to Himalayan trekking in the spring. The days are long, temperatures are warm, and the rhododendron trees are in full blossom. Our weather was outstanding while climbing to Kare Tal, the sacred Hindu lake. Clear skies and warm temperatures followed us all the way up the mountain. On reaching our destination at 4,500 metres Lynn, still full of energy and wanting to see more, suggested a further climb up a steep face above the lake for a view to Nilgiri and the Kali Gandaki gorge. It was late morning, and time was on our side. Happily, the rest of the group descended to our lunch destination located at our campsite from the night before, and Lynn and I spent the next half hour climbing to the knife-edge ridge. It was worth the effort as the view was spectacular. Far below, the tiny figures of our group worked their way slowly down the gorge to a well-earned lunch break.

It was then time to head down and meet the group below for lunch. As Lynn was descending at a faster rate, I described to her the location and asked her to look for the group near our campsite from the previous night. Once I arrived, perhaps 40 minutes later, I asked the sirdar about Lynn. She had not been seen – but this was not unusual. I assumed she had decided not to join the group for lunch and instead had carried on to the evening campsite by herself, which was a further 700 metres below.

I was soon to regret that assumption.

The route to our evening campsite was straightforward. It was a simple matter of following the ridge down to a tiny cluster of colourful tents below, etched against the skyline. To the right one could see a steep bowl-shaped couloir and the line of the forest trees 1,500 metres below, and to the left an uninviting rocky precipice. When we arrived at our campsite two hours later I asked a Sherpa guide if Lynn was in camp. "Not here," I was told.

I looked to the moonscape above and realized that she was somewhere back up the mountain and darkness was soon to be upon us. I was besieged with guilt. How could I have allowed myself to be so casual when as a leader my prime responsibility was client safety?

We started an immediate search. Two Sherpas quickly climbed back to our lunch spot in search of her. Later that evening they returned to camp, without good news. They had not found her.

Our rescue plan was to start our search at the first light of dawn. I would climb with three Sherpas to the ridge at 4,000 metres. The remaining group was to break camp and slowly begin the return trek to Pokhara.

With nighttime temperatures a few degrees below freezing, there was little else to think about: Lynn was lost on Annapurna South, and we had to find her.

At first light, we were up and away, and by mid-morning we were on the high ridge where we could see clearly both up and down the mountain. I thought that Lynn would be found somewhere at that elevation, having fallen and perhaps lying injured. At mid-morning, a Sherpa came to me with the news I was craving. Pointing down, with three unforgettable verbs that are seared into my memory, he said: "Mister Gordon, Mister Gordon – COME! LOOK! SEE!"

The Sherpa gestured and said, "THERE SHE IS – DOWN THERE!"

And there she was, 700 metres below us in the rocky couloir, just above the tree line – a small human speck in a red track suit climbing up through boulders. We sent her tumultuous calls of encouragement. And soon to our delight and great relief, she was back with us.

My first question was, "Lynn, how did you end up down there?"

Thinking she was on the trail to our previous lunch spot, she had turned right instead of left and drifted down the mountain into the couloir following an animal trail. Used to hiking alone, she thought nothing of strolling along until she realized she was seriously off course and lost. She then decided to descend further to the tree line and wait out the night, finding shelter under a rocky outcropping. The following morning, recognizing her mistake, she began her climb back up the mountain to the skyline ridge where we were standing.

Our small group returned to camp by noon hour to embraces and tears of delight. Night after night, the safe return of Lynn was celebrated. And I had learned another important lesson: Do not make decisions based on assumptions. Know the facts, then decide. It was to become a vital rule in our code of conduct for Everest Trekking.

Later in the trip when we were back in Kathmandu, one of the group reminded me of the dark moment when I had gathered the group in the dining tent to discuss the plans for the following day. He could not believe how calm I had appeared to them. I told him that he had not seen my shaking knees under the metal table.

There is a sequel to this story.

One year later, Lynn was returning to Kathmandu for another teaching assignment. She had been visiting family in Winnipeg; then flew to New York to stay with her daughter before flying on to Kathmandu via Pakistani Air. She was late arriving at the airport, and as the plane was overbooked, she was rebooked for the same flight the next day. Disappointed, she returned to her daughter's apartment.

The next morning Lynn called her mother to tell her about her change of plans and that she had not yet left. Her mother was speechless when she heard her daughter's voice. Lynn's mother then told her that the flight she was to have taken to Kathmandu had crashed with no survivors.

chapter 6

CLIMBING HIGH WITH THE NOMADS

1993 | GORD

The Seniors' Centre in West Vancouver was a favourite location for Everest Trekking slide shows and, surprisingly, a source of keen clients. One such group called themselves "the Nomads". They were a group of men in their 50s and 60s meeting regularly to run from the Centre along the seawall in West Vancouver. Their outstanding and irrepressible athletic leader was Frank.

Following our slide presentation, ten Nomads with a range of fitness levels signed up for a trek to Gokyo Ri and a visit to Tiger Tops Jungle Lodge in Chitwan National Forest. At our pre-trek briefing in the Kathmandu Guesthouse garden we had a weigh-in of trek bags to ensure that none exceeded the 15 kilo maximum limit. All bags passed the weight test except one. Albert's came in at 20 kilos. Examining his bag, Frank and I found that he had a sweet tooth. He had stashed five kilos of candy bars in his bag. After some discussion, it was agreed the bars would be left in a guesthouse locker. The following morning, as we were about to board the bus to catch our flight, Albert's bulging day bag caught my eye. Knowing that he could not afford anything more than the very minimum weight on his back, I said to Frank, "Look at this bag. We have a problem." Sure enough, there was most of the five kilos of candy. We persuaded Albert to save his strength and leave his candy behind, but for the next two weeks he never seemed to be short of treats, which he shared generously with the group.

Knowing the competitive nature of the Nomads, the trekking pace of the group was a hot topic. To ensure all remained healthy and strong, I emphasized the wisdom of walking slowly and hugging the mountainside of the trail when passing yak trains. It was apparent the next day that not everyone had been listening.

The following morning we flew by Twin Otter to Lukla, and our adventure began. After trekking for an hour we stopped for a rest to allow the group to come together. We realized that Albert was missing. A

Sherpa returned down the trail and soon found him. He had forgotten the warning about approaching yak trains, became caught on the outside, and was bunted off the trail by a particularly ornery beast. Fortunately the grade was not precipitous, and he didn't fall far. Other than a sprained finger and his damaged pride, he was not injured. Worse by far was the abuse he received from his fellow Nomads.

At Namche Bazar a day later, two trekkers were already showing signs of altitude sickness. They had slipped into "race mode", walked far too quickly, and suffered the consequences – splitting headaches and upset stomachs. Our planned day of rest at Namche Bazar was all that was needed for them to acclimatize, but it served notice to all that our climb ahead to Gokyo Ri at 5,340 metres deserved serious respect.

Our three-day climb to Gokyo went smoothly. The trek pace was measured and deliberate, and other than colds that spread through the group, our health was remarkable. Seven trekkers declared themselves ready on the eighth day for the early morning 700-metre ascent of Gokyo Ri. By now the pace had slowed to a crawl — heel to toe, heel to toe. We reached the peak in two hours and were rewarded with a stunning 360-degree panorama of Cho Oyu, Everest, Lhotse, and Makalu – four of the top ten mountains in the world.

On our descent to Namche Bazar, Bill became ill and was unable to climb one remaining pitch before an easy downhill to the village. We were faced with a steep and narrow trail up from the Phorste Tenga valley. He had to be carried on the back of Zambhu Sherpa, who weighed less than Bill.

A short pole was cushioned with foam rubber, and assembled by a Sherpa as a seat. A long strap was attached to each end of the pole to act as a tumpline around Bill's forehead, and as he rode high above Zambhu, the two began their tortuous climb up the switchback trail. It was a frightening sight to watch them – Zambhu cautiously feeling the rocky trail with his feet and Bill looking with apprehension to the valley below. Zambhu earned a large and appreciative tip that evening!

> RETURNING HOME TO NORMAL LIFE, THE NOMADS WOULD KNOW THAT AT THE EDGE OF UNCERTAINTY THERE IS ALWAYS ADVENTURE.

In spite of the high level of fitness, the group incurred an unusual number of ailments. Four suffered from altitude, four from gastro upset, nine from colds, and I developed an impacted tooth. Later I was treated at the dental clinic in Namche Bazar with a simple antibiotic. This ease of clinic access does not apply to those living in the remote regions of the Himalaya. In some cases, they suffer a lifetime of dental discomfort or chronic pain.

Many lessons were learned from this trek. There was to be no physical activity on our acclimatization day in Namche Bazar. In the future we would strictly enforce a maximum weight of five kilos or less for day bags and insist upon a relaxed and easy walking pace when we were above 3,000 metres. Invariably, trekkers walk too quickly on the first day. The excitement of finally being on the Himalayan trail after months of training at home generally translates into high-speed walking. The sky is blue, and the forest is green – all like home but the oxygen content of the air at 3,000 metres is a third less than at sea level, and the body responds accordingly.

Back in Namche Bazar we enjoyed beer and home-cooked meals once again. Shortly after our arrival Albert confessed that he had lost his camera. Convinced that he had left it by the trail earlier in the day, a Sherpa was sent with a handsome tip to find it. He did the return trip in two hours (it took us three hours one way) to return empty-handed. All eyes turned to Albert. Frank said, "Albert, give me your backpack." Sure enough, there was the camera, buried deep in the bag, hidden by candy bars. The Sherpa was delighted as he had just doubled his pay for the day for "a walk in the park", and the gang had another Albert tale to take home.

When we arrived in Lukla the weather looked uncertain for the following day, creating a concern about the flight to Kathmandu in the morning. Our worst fears were realized when we awoke to heavy fog. There were over 200 trekkers stranded, with the prospect of waiting days before flights resumed. The air of despondency descended like the fog. Later that morning, I was sitting at the edge of the runway when I heard my name: "Mister Gordon, Mister Gordon, helicopter below!" I couldn't believe what I was hearing!

Tashi, back in Kathmandu, and knowing of the closure at Lukla, called his friend and neighbour, Colonel Pun, who operated a helicopter mountain rescue service. Together they flew his sleek five-passenger Ecureuil helicopter to Surke, a tiny village located 550 metres directly below the Lukla airstrip.

The porters quickly gathered our duffle bags and jerry cans of extra fuel and danced down the steep trail into the fog. As I left, stranded trekkers were calling out to me, "Take me! Here's my $500. Come back for me!" We followed the porters in disbelief. Down and down we went, and as the fog thinned, we spotted the shiny body of the helicopter waiting in a potato field. Perched on a stone wall, casually drinking tea from a Chinese thermos, were Tashi and Colonel Pun.

In three successive flights, Colonel Pun flew us, with our duffle bags on our knees, down a narrow gorge to the small southern airstrip of Lami Danda. Within an hour we were together in the sunshine at this remote airstrip, only to be told once again that there were no scheduled flights that day.

However, Tashi had worked his magic with a chartered flight from Kathmandu, and moments later we heard the sound of an approaching aircraft. A Dornier STOL aircraft circled the field once, touched down, and taxied up to our group. The cabin door swung open and, like a vision from heaven, there appeared a flight attendant holding a full box of beer on ice.

The return flight to Kathmandu was wild and raucous. We had dodged a three-day wait in Lukla. The boys were going home! Many rousing toasts were made to Tashi who had provided us with an incomparable Khumbu experience. Returning home to normal life, the Nomads would know that at the edge of uncertainty there is always adventure.

chapter 7

THE "OH MY GOD" GROUP

1994 | GAIL

Phaplu is a collection of medieval houses clustered on a hillside in eastern Nepal. Where the dirt airstrip slashed across terraced fields of millet, a small crowd of villagers huddled on the slope, eager to witness the ungainly hulk of our Russian Mi-17 helicopter landing on a small marked patch of ground. The propellers stirred up a mini dust storm as we touched down, and the deafening noise inside the stripped-down interior faded. We could then remove the tufts of cotton from our ears, undo the restraining wire across our collective laps, and ease our way along the steel benches. With some relief, we tumbled down the metal steps, happy not to be combat soldiers with guns at the ready, but merely a clutch of placid seniors blinking in the afternoon light.

Ang Nuri, our Nepalese leader, was waiting for us among the villagers with his staff of porters, kitchen boys, and Sherpa guides. As his eyes scanned the group, he moaned audibly. "Oh my God, how am I going to herd these old people up to 4,000 metres?"

There was no question that these nine trekkers were old. Their average age was seventy-two. They were coping with various physical challenges such as hearing loss, the lifelong effects of childhood polio, and lower back pain. At seventy-seven, Ian could stand or lie down, but sitting was painful because of his artificial hips. What were they doing here? Most people at their age want comfy beds, three-star hotels, hot baths, clean clothes, and predictable travel experiences. Not this group! They wanted adventure.

"We could die on this trip," Mary said, "but we could die looking out our apartment window at home too." *Carpe diem* was their mantra. In the Vancouver airport departure lounge we had sat among a large group of seniors on their way to a cruise around the South China Sea. With their names hanging from tags on their necks, they looked like aged Paddington Bears. Forbes, who was 75, confessed "You know

Gail, I'm saving that kind of holiday for when I'm old."

I was to be seriously humbled by these outstanding people.

The Namche Hill was to be their biggest challenge. Frank, one of their younger friends from the West Vancouver Seniors Centre, a 63-year-old long-distance runner, had achieved this goal the year before. He told them they'd never make it up that hill. "Forget it!" he advised. "Forget the whole idea. It's too damn tough."

On the seventh day of the trek they were faced with the famous steep 700-metre trail that snaked up the mountain unrelentingly, at times no wider than a goat track. An admiring German trekker complimented one of our 73-year-olds. He declared, "You're really tough!" Jean later heartily agreed. "I thought I was going to die going up that hill."

The glow of pride from such a "nothing ventured, nothing gained" achievement lingered long after sunset that evening as we all collapsed by the charcoal fire in Tashi's family lodge.

We were privileged to be lodged at Phurdiki and Ang Pasang's family home, the oldest in Namche Bazar. Their private gompa was filled with ancient sacred books bound in wood to protect the hand-printed pages. Hammered gold and silver water urns, carpets, and conch shells were scattered around the room, while candles and offerings of rice to their golden Buddha filled every shelf. This was a temple of daily worship seldom seen by a Westerner. We had the good luck to be here for Dorje and Ang Maya's birthday party for their year-old son, Phinzo. The Sherpanis, dressed in their long skirts, woven aprons, and turquoise and gold earrings, gossiped in their soft Tibetan dialect while nursing their babes or cradling them while they slept in their arms. The potent mountain beer flowed freely. Outside, the snow-fluted mountains mirrored the moonlight, and stars were an arm's length away. It was enough to forge a romantic out of the most hardened cynic.

That was our lodge night but the rest of the nights were spent in tents. Dorothy, almost 76, commented, "You know, I've never slept in a tent and I love it. Now I know I can do the Tatshenshini River in Yukon." The next year, she rafted the white-water river with confidence. She also had advice for anyone travelling while leaving grown children behind. "I lined up all the shoes in my cupboard, so if I didn't return, my daughter-in-law wouldn't say, 'Look at that jumble of shoes. It just shows her chaotic way of thinking.'"

Ever since then I never go on a trip without organizing my shoes in perfect rows, and I always think of Dorothy.

One lovely day, sitting in the sun after lunch listening to yak bells and the whistles of their drivers, Max sighed. "When it's like this, you could live another hundred years." Meanwhile, he and the others were getting the most out of their first hundred. They all worked at being in good shape and claimed that life is more enjoyable when you are fit. It was forbidden to discuss ailments. Vitamins yes, but no "organ recitals". Beryl, the youngest of the group at 60, thought that hiking was the best thing she had ever discovered. They all believed that muscles stiffen and atrophy if they aren't used. Physically prepared for the challenges of this journey, and laughing at the skeptics, they knew they were mentally primed to succeed. This must be the secret to living a long time without growing old.

At Tengboche monastery, 700 metres above Namche Bazar, the monks were preparing for Mani Rimdu, their annual religious festival. We watched three of them, crouched on carpets, laboriously tapping coloured grains of sand through a copper funnel onto a square wooden surface. They were creating the geometric designs of a mandala – an aid used to focus the mind. Two hundred hours of labour would later be destroyed in a trice during a ceremony that highlighted the Buddhist truth – change is inevitable and attachment to beauty is ephemeral. While this may be true, the Sherpas have no word in their language for stress or depression, and I could understand why. They live among the thrones of their mountain gods, steeped in spirituality.

Ang Nuri never told us about his "Oh My God" comment until we were at Dingboche and 4,300 metres. Here, he confessed his reservations. He shook his head in admiration and told the group that, as far as he knew, they were the oldest to ever achieve that elevation in the Everest region. The seniors proudly named themselves the "Oh My God group", impressing the tough Sherpas with their optimism and extraordinary mental strength.

> MAYBE WE SHOULD HAVE GONE ON THAT LUXURY CRUISE WITH PERCY AND NEIL.
>
> *- Dorothy, age 75*

From the height of Dingboche to the jungle is as big a change as you can imagine, travelling from dry cold air and barren rocks to lush jungle foliage and heat. We all went down to Chitwan National Park, where the group rode elephants and saw rhinos and deer and crocodiles and many species of water birds. Dorothy felt ill from facing backwards on her elephant howdah. In her journal, she wrote of a remark she made to Forbes, her companion, "Maybe we should have gone on that luxury cruise with Percy and Neil."

Her words to all of us at the final dinner were, "This trip is one I will never forget. It was darn hard work, but magnificent." Some of the group said it was the best experience of their lives.

GORD

I was trekking with a group to Gokyo at the time the OMG group was on their way to Namche Bazar. We had reached the summit of Gokyo, and the prospect of returning to the luxury of Camp de Base in Namche Bazar was dancing in our heads. Hot showers and a warm dining room were the lead topic of conversations as we descended from the thin air of the high Khumbu. Three days later, in the late afternoon, we were looking down on the village and the roof of Phurdiki and Ang Pasang's house.

If everything went according to plan, our group was to arrive at the same time as Gail's. Was this possible? It was an eight-day trek from Phaplu to Namche with a cumulative climb of over 3,300 metres. Could these people of advanced age achieve such a goal? Would they be felled by altitude sickness or colds or gastro problems? Would Loretta with her walking sticks and raised boot, due to childhood polio, be able to adapt to the rugged trail? And Ian, with his two artificial hips, would he be too exhausted to continue? All these concerns ran through my head as I approached the lodge.

The living room of the lodge faced south and overlooked the village below. I stepped into the room, and there they were – all smiles with tanned faces and a light in their eyes. They had achieved what many had thought impossible, and they exuded a youthful pride. From Namche Bazar, they continued on to Tengboche Monastery, camped in the snow, and reached their goal of "going high and seeing Everest".

No sissy-trip for the "Oh My Gods."

Back in Vancouver, we continued to do our promotional Himalayan trek slide shows. And as long as we showed our slides, we had a guaranteed audience from the OMGs. They were our finest example of the saying, "The difference between an adventure and an ordeal is attitude!"

chapter 8

JEWELWEED AND ELEPHANTS

GORKHA/CHITWAN

1992 | GAIL

Kipling wrote "the wildest dreams of Kew are the facts of Khatmandhu" and Bill, a Vancouver dentist, had to agree as he stared at the toothache tree near the Durbar Square in Kathmandu. If you banged a nail into the wood, your toothache would go away. Really! The block of wood was covered in nails. That could have meant either a lot of toothaches or a lot of hoped-for miracle cures. Bill was keen to trek with his wife, Lois, and their two daughters, ages 12 and 16.

A seven hour bus trip brought us to the head of the trail at the village of Gorkha. One night the girls asked Rinzi, our sirdar, how many children he had. We were sitting in a tent by the lantern light, high on a hill in the Gorkha area. Rinzi, one arm flung over the shoulder of our Sherpa cook, Maila, shrugged. "Eight," he said. "Next year – huh, maybe nine." The girls were wide-eyed.

Early in the trek, one of our clients slipped and sprained her ankle. Her friend remained with her, and they left with a porter carrying her on his back. Raj was a heavy woman weighing far more than the slender porter, but with a tumpline over his forehead and around her buttocks, he managed to carry her like a plank for most of a day.

At our high point, Serandanda, villagers came to sing and dance for us. Maila, the cook, taught us how to make delicate Tibetan dumplings called Momos for dinner. We toured the high village the next day and watched animal skins being stretched to use as hinges for the villagers' plows. A woman sat weaving a basket nearby, and her young son solemnly shook a trekker's hand in thanks for the Band-Aid he received for his cut finger. As we descended to the Marsyangdi River, the mountains provided a cool backdrop for fields of yellow flowers and spring green rice paddies.

Dwight, a Shanghai-born medical doctor with a balance problem, shouted out, "Take my picture! My wife will never believe I'm doing this," as he clutched the hand of his Sherpa and carefully picked his way down a steep stony slope. At the end of our trip, Dwight wrote in his diary, "I think this has been one of the crowning achievements of my life!" Here was a man with several medical degrees and many awards and honours to his name. He was a published author and a senior cardiologist in Canada, and he was glowing over this as his peak experience.

For the next two days we rafted the Trisuli River, swam at lunchtime, and camped for the night on a sandbar. It was a grade-three river with some rapids, but not too frightening. We passed river festivals where marigolds were tossed into the current with the hope that they would eventually float to the Ganges.

A bus picked us up by the road on the second day and we followed the river down to the high luxury of Tiger Tops Jungle Resort in Chitwan National Park. This park was created in 1962 and became a national park in 1973. It covers 930 square kilometres. There were 800 military personnel guarding the park from rhino poaching, a constant problem. Eighty Bengal tigers and over 500 rhinos inhabited this wildlife refuge.

Where the river slowed and widened, we crossed in a flat boat past a Gharial fish-eating crocodile lazing on an island in the sun. Staff greeted us in jeeps for the ride to the lodge. Tiger Tops had three locations – Tharu Village located on the outskirts of the park, the Main Lodge within the boundaries, and the Tented Camp situated deeper in the jungle. Sixty guests were cared for by a staff of over 200, many being naturalists.

Our first night was at the Tharu Village, where we were entertained with Tharu cultural dancing. In the morning some of us rode polo ponies in the mist through rice fields. Polo is a popular sport, sometimes played on elephants on the air strip.

The Main Lodge had a capacity of 35 guests. Nearby, Tiger Tops' 13 elephants were housed. Each elephant was partnered with a mahout, and the two were inseparable. The elephants were bathed every day in the river, a necessary and popular ritual and grand spectacle for the guests. We became friendly with a couple of them, feeding them balls of rolled up grass.

Later we had the thrill of lumbering along in a howdah high above the elephant grass. Twice a day, we ventured into the high grass on the backs of elephants in search of the one-horned rhinoceros and barking deer. We saw tiger tracks, but no tiger. They are nocturnal hunters, and by nighttime we would be tucked into our tent in the Tented Camp, deep in the jungle.

The Tented Camp was located on the edge of the river basin, deep in the park, and it could shelter 16 guests in eight high-end tents. A viewing platform along the ridge in front of the tents provided a place to sit with a cold drink and watch rhinoceros and sometimes even gaur or Indian Bison graze on the grasslands below.

One of my most memorable experiences was listening to the music of the jungle lying in my comfortable cot with a hot water bottle, tent flap closed, and coal oil lantern burning outside to keep wildlife away. There was a feeling of peace amid the threat of the unknown in these strange surroundings. In the morning, condensation from overnight fog dripped on the tent and signalled the start of another day.

In 2014, the park was closed to overnight accommodation. The Tiger Tops lease on the land inside the park expired, and the government had no interest in renewing it. This magical destination is now a dream.

ROCKSLIDES AND EYELASHES

1994 | GORD

Our third Gorkha/Chitwan trek was scheduled during the cooler temperatures of early November. We were an eclectic group from Vancouver, Toronto and Washington State. The trek started off with a mishap. We had walked from the Kathmandu Guest House just after breakfast to meet our bus near the King's Palace. The streets were teeming with workers and students, and when we reached our appointed street corner, the bus had yet to arrive. Norman, from Toronto, decided to hang his day backpack on a metal fence while he tied his shoelace. When he turned around to reach for his bag, it was gone. Panic! We spread out to search for the backpack with no luck. In a trice, he had lost his camera, wind jacket, water bottle and warmest sweater. Fortunately, we were going to a warm climate and needed only the bare essentials to get through the day. Norman's solution – a garbage bag tied to his waist as a backpack, while not fashionable, was certainly functional.

The next day, the bus trip to Gorkha, normally a three-hour journey, was delayed by a massive rockslide on the road. As with all road repairs in Nepal, manual work to clear the road would take a week, so the Nepalis quickly solved the problem by switching buses on opposite sides of the slide. We crawled over the debris with our porters and all our gear and exchanged buses with passengers going in the other direction. By sunset, we had arrived at the town of Gorkha, home of the world-renowned Gurkha soldiers.

This trek required only the lightest of clothing. The temperature ranged between 10 and 28 degrees. Shorts were worn in the daytime, and a light fleece was perfect for evening. The air was heavy and sweet compared to the thin air of the Khumbu. We walked for seven to eight hours each day, developed a hearty appetite for dinner, and filled the time in the evenings with a rousing card game of Hearts. As the dining tent served as the bedroom for staff, we were early to bed most nights by eight o'clock.

The first night, the location of the tents was an issue. Nicole, our high-maintenance fashionista, had a change of clothes for each day. One of 17 children from a Quebec family, she was the only one to leave the province and head to the West Coast to become a successful real estate agent billed as "The French Connection." She insisted on a tent location well away from the group. The leader prevailed, and the tents remained together. "But Gordon...they snore!" she complained. Each morning, Nicole was the last to come to breakfast. It took time for make up perfection and false eyelash attachments.

Although she was unable to swim, she joined us on the raft for two days. I sat directly behind her for both days. We changed position in the raft every half hour, and Nicole did not flinch when it was her time to sit in the front seat. That meant taking on the full force of the water when we hit major waves. When the going got rough, I hung on to her life vest. It wasn't long before she took a solid wave in her face. When the water cleared, her makeup was running down her face, but her eyelashes were still in place. "Nicole, your eyelashes – they're still there."

She exclaimed triumphantly, "Oh Gor-don, they are glued on."

We celebrated our rafting experience with a gourmet meal on a sand beach by the edge of the river. The following morning, we boarded a bus and descended to the Chitwan National Forest and the famed Tiger Tops Jungle Lodge.

On one evening safari, I shared an elephant with Nicole. There were six elephants in our group directed by the headman, who was standing on the back of our elephant and holding on to the howdah. With his sharp eyes, he picked up the telltale paw prints of a tiger, and the hunt began. Soon he organized the elephants to encircle a dense growth of tall grass where he suspected the tiger was hiding. The closer the circle was tightened, the unhappier the elephants became. Suddenly, the tiger bolted from the grass directly below us. In his panic to flee, he jumped at our elephant wounding his ear before disappearing. In the melee, we hung on as our elephants lurched and trumpeted. Nicole was the toast of the lodge on our return, having survived a wild ride.

THE LAUGHING DIDIS OF GORKHA

1995 | GAIL

"WELCOME MR GORDON KONANTZ AND GUESTS" announced the banner. The sign spanned the entire facade of the Kathmandu Guest House in recognition of the eight years we had been coming to this beloved budget hotel. We so appreciated this complimentary gesture by the management who had become our friends.

We arrived in sheets of rain, a late monsoon, and this time several of our groups happened to be there at the same time before scattering through the Himalaya or travelling home. Sloshing through puddles, we met for dinner and compared adventures.

The next morning rain continued as we drove for almost six hours to the trailhead. Steep drop-offs and slick mud presented a wide array of accidents – three bus pile-ups and assorted vehicles abandoned in ditches and at the bottom of gullies. Mugling, where we stopped for lunch, was choked with transport buses and littered with garbage and orange peels. By the time we got to the trail head at Dumre there was already talk of a plan B, bailing or bed, and we had yet to leave our hard bus seats and enter the downpour and mud. Laurie, our witty trekker, quipped, "I've always wanted to go to Dumre and buy an umbrella in the rain. Why it just doesn't get any better!"

Starting off uphill, long-sleeved tops and warm pants in 100% humidity became an instant bad idea. We were soaked from the inside out as we carefully placed our feet to avoid the slurry of mud slopped over the stones. By the time we arrived at our campsite the tents were barely outlined in the fog and rain. Sherpas were digging trenches to divert the water. And there were the leeches that always come with rain. These tiny vampire-worms sneak silently under your clothes and attach themselves to your skin. Three of us already had blood in our socks.

But then, lanterns snuffed out, it was time to listen to the rain falling softly on the tent. We were dry inside. The music of Nepali voices and the clang of dishes sloshing in pans of water filled the air. I gathered in my thoughts the lovely sights, smells and sounds of the day – wood smoke, bougainvillea in bloom, a bell sounding in a temple, children calling "Namaste", a radio playing Indian music, voices in a foreign tongue. All this made me happy to be back and crowded out any negative moments.

One night we camped by a river and the owner of the land came by for donations to the local school. He remembered our group from two years earlier when we gave them all the clothes we could, and he remarked that his wife was wearing one of our shawls from that time. She and their four children stood by smiling.

Our longest day was hot and tough. No one talked. We stopped many times and were passed by the porters carrying knee-buckling loads. Many of them were from farms in the area. They had an air of elegance in their ragged clothes with Kukri knives tucked in their belt straps. Boiled wool rugs of burnt sienna covered their shoulders. Making extra money working for a trekking group added to their meagre income.

"NAMASTE, NAMASTE" RANG THROUGH THE HILLS. REFRESHED ON COLD BEER AND HOT TANG WE SLIPPED AND WE SLITHERED AND TOTTERED AND TRUDGED. THEN WE SKIPPED AND WE STRODE AND WE SANG.

– Debbie Riley

After a three-hour slog uphill, we collapsed under a Peepal tree. Like filings to a magnet, children gathered to point and gawk at two of us who were curled on a mat in the fetal position, feeling so sick. Goats bleated nearby, and a small puppy snooped about looking for scraps.

All afternoon we climbed – endlessly up. I was starting to think this was a big mistake when suddenly we stumbled upon our tents set in a broad meadow. They were facing Manaslu and the setting sun. This was our most spectacular campsite. Dinner of pizza and spring rolls with tomato sauce was greeted with rounds of applause. Children came to sing and dance for us. They were from four to thirteen years in age, and we were the ones longing for bedtime. But no, after sitting in rows, downing cups of beer, the Memsahibs were dragged to the lantern light to dance with the cook and the sirdar, the village men, and with each other. They called us Didis, which meant older sisters and gestured to the star-studded sky while the surrounding mountains glowed in their light.

The next morning we hiked through fields of yellow mustard and picked branches of jewelweed whose seeds exploded when you touched them. But sadly the closer we walked to the road and our waiting bus, the nastier the children became. They grabbed at our packs and put hands in front of our faces, begging for pens or gum or even money. This was the result of too many foreign tourists' misguided actions.

On our last night, we held our traditional Everest Trekking ceremony, with money for the porters, a raksi drinking party, and tips all around. Piling up our unwanted gear, we made the mistake of not letting the lesser-paid porters choose first. As a result the Sherpas who always began first took most of the expensive equipment such as Thermarest mattresses and fleeces, leaving nothing but ball caps and t-shirts for the porters.

A hot three-hour trip took us down to the jungle and Tiger Tops Lodge. At the tented camp, the staff discreetly warned us about "mice" that had been nibbling at the tents. I was nervously alone in my tent at

the end of the row, and these were not innocent little mice, they were bamboo rats. That night, I awoke with a start to hear a roar and the breaking of sticks. Not a rat, but far more frightening – a tiger. My naïve thoughts of the peace of the jungle were shattered by white fear as I clutched my hot-water bottle and imagined the claw of a tiger and the flimsy canvas of my tent. But we were safe. The tigers in the park were named and counted, and this was Rue Poti, the female tiger with her three cubs. The sound of breaking sticks frightened her into leaving the area – or so the "mouse warners" assured us.

Back in Kathmandu the group shopped and ate in funky restaurants like the Dechen Ling Garden in the heart of Thamel, and Fire and Ice, a pizza joint run by an Italian from Naples. They bought carpets in Patan at the Tibetan Refugee Camp and then allowed all their senses to be overwhelmed by burning bodies, chaotic colours, and the cacophony of sounds at Shiva's Pashupatinath Temple. We stood across the river from corpses being burned on tall funeral pyres, as chanting white-clad mourners solemnly circled the flames. This public display was unheard-of in our world. I don't even know where bodies are taken before cremation in Canada. All is hidden, as though death is a rare event.

Ashes were dumped into the garbage-filled Bagmati river in hopes that they would float the deceased's soul to the holy Ganges and finally to the sea. We encountered monkeys, haggard holy cows, hawkers peddling pots of coloured dyes, flute players, and ash-smeared Sadhu priests chanting pujas, all steeped in the smell of incense mixed with urine. When a leper danced by on his hands, waving the stumps of his legs in our faces, of one of our group moaned, "I can hardly WAIT to get home."

From the gratitude of a farmer to the grace of a Namaste greeting, we all agreed our view of the world had expanded in surprising ways.

IN THEIR VOICES – THE DIDIS REMINISCE

This spontaneous thread of emails led to a coming of age party in the summer of 2016. Every summer our Gorkha trip is celebrated, but twenty-one was special. Momos and margaritas were featured, we sang, we gathered by the light of the moon and told tales of when we were all together so long ago.

From Didi Joan

I am in Inchon Airport Lounge waiting for my flight to Myanmar. I started to think back on all my trips, and my first with those adventurous Didis was still my favourite. I cannot stop thinking about some of the stuff we did on that trip.

Do you remember singing karaoke at the hotel in Hong Kong, the bus ride down to the harbour (some of us could not remember the last time we had been on public transportation), Dim Sum, paying extra to get into Nepal but Debbie wanting her money back, the sometimes hot water at the Kathmandu Guest House, the YAK YAK YAK t-shirts, the stupas, buying pillow covers at the back of our tour group, the restaurant for lunch on the way to Pokhara, its "bathroom", buying the umbrellas, walking up the mountain at dusk in the rain, chatter from one tent about Plan B – back to Kathmandu to shop, the leeches, waking up the next day above the clouds, sliding down the mountain the next day, our leader curled up in the fetal position beside the trail, Carol and her zip lock bags, a little up – a little down – a little along, only up, marigolds everywhere, the huge brown eyes of the children, the water system, the vibrant green of the terraced rice fields, dancers at night, 10 years on a stair climber, walking in front of the Annapurnas, the school, large beers, the swing bridge, Debbie V. buying a cow, elephant rides, jungle rats eating the hearing aids, the tiger growling in the night, playing football on the runway with the kids, the smoking section on a plane, teaching the Japanese to use child-proof lighters, dents in the plane, and so much laughter. My list is incomplete.

I have not included the whole cultural experience and the beauty and kindness of the Nepalese people we met as we trekked through their villages. It was all magical 20 years ago, and it cemented our friendship.

From Didi Laurie

At the moment, I'm having breakfast in Samarkand, Uzbekistan and keep thinking of the line in Debbie Riley's poem that we would follow our intrepid leader Gail to Samarkand! And here I am. Did no one mention the charpi yet? Perhaps just as well. One of my absolute favorite memories is of dancing madly under the light of the full moon on the top of the world – whirling dervishes indeed. And what about the little kids crowding around to look at the pictures in the magazines? I remember the runny little noses and shining eyes and giggles.

Did our cook make a birthday cake on the open stove?

Am I dreaming when I remember a seemingly treacherous swinging bridge at the end of our trek and the amazing bus journey to Tiger Tops and having a REAL shower and luxuriating between clean sheets in a real bed? And did our jeep get stuck in the mud in the forest beside some tiger tracks as the sun was setting, or did I just imagine that?

Is it all a beautiful dream?

From Didi Gail (the Tall One)

You did forget the post-trek giant beers in Nepal – one was enough to get Debbie R and me tipsy, but that might not be saying much. I still salivate while remembering garlic soup with its garnish of popcorn followed by singing didis and bobbing headlamps. Nepal trip is numero UNO for me as well. You, Gail, Debbie, Carol, Debbie, Laurie, Trish, and Donna were great "road" companions. Has anybody had bed tea since? Remember all the smiling faces that greeted us all day long, joyful really – blisters and moleskin aside. Best walk of my life to date!

These are friendships and memories to treasure.

chapter 9

TIBET

WHEN THE IRON BIRD FLIES

1995 | GORD

In May of 1995 I travelled from Kathmandu to Lhasa in an '86 Toyota Land Cruiser, the vehicle of choice in a land unfriendly to modern machines. Sharing this epic trip across the roof of the world with me was our partner, Tashi, and John, a friend from Vancouver. Dirt roads often had uneven surfaces, or they were nothing more than tire tracks across the land. Service stations were unknown. As gasoline was available only at a few major centres, we carried reserve fuel with us. The driver and his friend beside him in the front seat did all mechanical repairs.

Prior to departing, John and I spent two weeks in the lush Solu district exploring a new trek route to the base of Mount Numbur. While waiting for our Twin Otter to leave the Kathmandu domestic terminal, we ordered hot cereal with milk. Fifteen hours later, we discovered to our discomfort that the milk was bad, an oversight that would have repercussions for the next three weeks. This was not a good beginning for our travels into the remote backcountry of Solu, where a strong stomach was a priority.

A half-day drive from Kathmandu to the Tibetan border ended at the Nepali village of Kodari. There we hired a truck to take us eight kilometres up an extremely rough mountain road to reach the border and the village of Zhangmu. I remarked in my journal, "It was a trip from hell with forty-five minutes of grinding gears, black exhaust fumes, and many refills of the radiator."

Our truck was stopped at the border by a Chinese official dressed in cowboy boots and a ball cap. Slouching in a garden chair, he rudely demanded our passports, gave them a cursory glance, and ordered us to return in the morning. Although it was mid-afternoon we had arrived "after hours". All of Tibet was on Beijing time.

Zhangmu was a squalid assortment of dilapidated shacks scattered along the side of a hill. It was a typical road terminus – a commercial sinkhole, a clutter of trucks and traders, moneychangers, and hookers. Half-built structures were surrounded by garbage. Our hotel had all the charm of an army barracks. There was no hot water, and the iron springs poking through the worn mattresses made sleeping all but impossible.

We met our two Tibetan drivers at the hotel. They were in their early twenties, and the driver, who wore white gloves, displayed a certain swagger. He was a good driver – and he knew it. Travel time each day was limited to six hours due to the dust and rough terrain. I quickly discovered the reason for the two handles next to the rear doors. It was imperative to hold onto both – at all times. Three of us sat in the rear seat, and the person in the middle wrapped a sleeping bag around his shoulders to soften the body blows. We didn't eat much at breakfast or lunch, as it was impossible to digest food properly with all the shaking and dust.

The road from Zhangmu to the first major pass, the Tong La, climbs 3,000 metres over 95 kilometres from forest to dry desert land. Upon reaching the summit of the pass we gingerly stepped out of the car for partial views of Shishapangma, Cho Oyu, and the barren moonscape to the north. The mountains dominated the horizon. Everest Base Camp was our destination the next day.

We stayed overnight in Tingri, a gas depot village, in a motel-type structure without floors. The following morning we set off across the rolling hills and the Pang La, to the Rongbuk Monastery for lunch, the last human settlement before base camp. The monastery had been destroyed by the Chinese and recently had been partially rebuilt by the few remaining monks. This was the home of Tucci Rinpoche, who fled to the Solu Khumbu, Nepal to found the Tubten Choling Monastery near Junbesi, now a thriving teaching centre with over 300 monks.

It is a 15-kilometre drive from Rongbuk to Everest Base Camp where we set up our tents for a cold night at 5,100 metres. We couldn't help but think of the epic journeys of British expeditions in the 1920s and their months of walking from Darjeeling to reach this same campsite.

The following day, we retraced our route toward Tingri and headed east to Lhatse, where we found a hotel that rivalled that of Zhangmu. We were still suffering from queasy stomachs, and the bumpy roads and grim Tibetan fare added to our misery.

Our hotel in Lhatse was on the main street, which also served as the trans-Tibetan highway. The street was torn up and was being rebuilt by hand. We were on the second floor overlooking the work when a dust storm swept in from the west. Workers covered themselves as best they could and carried on digging or pounding rocks. The hotel, perhaps ten years old, was spartan, yet relatively clean. Our hot water came from the kitchen and as was the custom it was dumped out the window when we finished with it. Dinner in our room was a bowl of noodles and some steamed rice. We found some buns at a grimy restaurant across the street.

The night was long and uncomfortable, a now recurring and familiar theme. As the mattress spring stuck into my back, I inflated my air mattress to make the bed more comfortable. The wind continued to blow, so we had to keep our window closed. Still we could hear people singing and shouting, dogs barking, and trucks changing gears well into the night. Drunks roamed the hallway and tried our door.

I slept fitfully and dreamed of sailing on Lake of the Woods, sweet visions making up for our squalid surroundings. The following morning we ate breakfast across the street in an unheated room with a few metal tables. We sat opposite a Tibetan family who were fascinated with the appearance of two westerners and a Sherpa. It wasn't long before Tashi began to laugh. One of the Tibetans had said, "Look, the old man is sick." They were right; I was both aged and sick.

The country was transformed the next morning. The air was still and clear following the night rain. Spring planting was in full swing across the brown fields, and the sky was cobalt blue. Two yaks pulled a plow, followed by a child sprinkling seeds.

The road soon began to climb to another pass at 4,500 metres, and the valley on the other side revealed a timeless scene – more fields being ploughed with yaks, a small village with colourful prayer flags fluttering, water canals, children playing, and all surrounded by low, brown hills.

Coloured prayer flags were everywhere in Tibet. They flew from poles in courtyards, horizontally above buildings, and on bridges. Each flag was imprinted with the Buddhist mantra, *Om Mani Padme Hum* (Praise to the Jewel in the Heart of the Lotus), and the breeze would scatter the prayers throughout the land. The five colours of the flags represented essential elements: blue (sky), white (clouds), red (fire), green (water), and yellow (earth).

After four hours of bone-rattling dusty travel we reached Shigatse and checked into a newly built Chinese hotel complete with essential facilities: running water, a good kitchen, and comfortable beds. Tashi's fame as leader of the Tibetan-Nepali Everest climbing team in 1988 had preceded him. The following day we joined him for a luncheon held in his honour by the mayor of the city. We were treated

Fort Gyantse

Potala Palace

to a premium Tibetan meal: eight courses of yak beginning with the tongue and finishing with the tail. Each course was another organ delicacy. As we bravely picked through the meal, I leaned over to Tashi and whispered to him, "When will this end, Uncle Tashi?" "When the soup comes, Uncle Gord," he assured me. It couldn't have come quickly enough. We referred to each other with this honorific phrase for fun, and we both loved it.

Tashilhunpo, Tibet's largest and most active monastery, had about 800 resident monks at the time. The monastery was founded in 1447 and was built on a hill in central Shigatse. The feature building was the Maitrya Temple (Jamba Chyenmu), built in 1914 by the Ninth Panchen Lama, to house the gigantic Maitrya Buddha containing 279 kilograms of gold. We entered the murky interior with the usual flow of pilgrims, to be faced with a wrought-iron fence, masses of butter lamps, and the feet of a towering Buddha. Monks chanted, and the air was rich with the smell of incense and hot yak butter burning in small containers. Slowly we lifted our eyes to take in this massive 26-metre figure towering over us. We felt humbled and overwhelmed by the devotion of the pilgrims who pressed around us.

The 10th Panchen Lama died in 1989, and his reincarnation was discovered in 1995. The Chinese had removed him just prior to our arrival. Heavily armed soldiers patrolled our surroundings and a sense of gloom and depression filled the air. We were advised to not ask political questions because spies were everywhere.

We travelled on to Gyantse, two hours east of Shigatse, to visit the Kumbum, the largest chorten in the country. Its 77 chapels on six floors were decorated with over 10,000 murals. The monastery suffered heavy damage during the Cultural Revolution, and it was now virtually empty of monks. Of the original eighteen buildings in the complex, only three remained.

East of Gyantse, we stopped for a picnic near Yamdrok Tso, the largest lake in Southern Tibet. Revered as part of the life-spirit of the Tibetan nation, it is said that if its waters dry up, Tibet will no longer be habitable.

We arrived at the summit of the Kyoga La at 4,900 metres where four small girls mysteriously appeared seemingly out of nowhere. We were delighted that we could give them our remaining food.

Our first distant sighting of Lhasa was the iconic Potala Palace. Lhasa lies at the east end of a long valley, and the Potala Palace dominates the skyline. It was built in 1645 on the Marpo Ri ridge nearly 300 metres above the city. With more than 1,000 rooms, 10,000 shrines, and over 200,000 statues, it had been the residence of the Dalai Lama and the Tibetan seat of power until the country was over-run by the Chinese in 1959.

After driving 1,186 kilometres in seven days over inhospitable terrain, and crossing seven major passes, we were relieved to luxuriate in the comfort of the Lhasa Holiday Inn. On this journey we had witnessed many wonders: chanting monks in red robes; prayer flags on high passes; a yak skin boat on a turquoise lake; glorious 15th century paintings in a mandala-shaped temple; small horses threshing grain or pulling entire families to market, hitched to two-wheeled carts; and always the smiling faces of the Tibetan people. The contrast between the Tibetans and the Chinese was palpable, and it was difficult not to make comparisons – hospitable and warm versus stern and cold, colourful and spiritual versus drab and practical.

Tibetan women in Lhasa are beautiful. They circled the Jokhang temple spinning prayer wheels, with turquoise jewels and silver strands twined into their shiny black braids. Men wore multi-coloured hand-woven cloaks lined in lambskin. We felt we had been transported back on a magic carpet to the exotic 10th- century pilgrimages that we read about in storybooks.

Temple roofs, sheathed in gold with dharma wheels and snow lion gargoyles, glimmered in the sun. Inside this most sacred Tibetan temple, ochre, red, maroon, vermilion, and gold colours surrounded us, and Buddhas glowed in the soft light of hundreds of butter lamps. Brightly painted wrathful gods evoked thoughts of Last Judgments in French Romanesque churches. The devoted pilgrims prostrated themselves before their deities on paving stones worn into deep furrows by the thousands who came before them. They brushed by us, making their offerings of butter, silk scarves, and money, touching their foreheads to the base of the gods in respect.

Lhasa felt like an occupied city. A heavy military presence, restricted travel, and the limited use of monasteries created an undercurrent of sadness among the local people. More than a million Tibetans had been killed since the Chinese invaded Tibet in 1959 and the Dalai Lama fled the country. At this time schoolchildren were being taught in Chinese. Monks had been removed from now-almost-empty monasteries. Surveillance cameras lined rooftops. Tibetans were so restricted in their activities that they were forbidden to talk publicly in groups of more than two people. Now dominated by the Chinese, Tibetans felt they were treated like cattle.

We were reminded of the prediction made by Padmasambhava, the Guru Rinpoche of the 8th century:

Tashilhumpo Monastery

SOLDIERS AND SPIRITS UNBOWED

1996 | GAIL

After my trip to Copra Ridge I travelled to Tibet to join a group of friends. Leaving Kathmandu I flew by the green folded hills of Nepal and the jagged white peaks of the Himalaya. Everest was within touching distance as our plane banked around it, and soon the ground colours changed from lush green to the rain-deprived dun of the Tibetan plateau. Beyond the mountains the flat plateau appeared like a child's project in papier-mâché.

Beside a river in the middle of nowhere, we landed at the Lhasa airport. We were the only aircraft to land on the one runway. Chinese army guards stood in random spots like cardboard cutouts. We drove for an hour and a half to Lhasa. Along the way we saw no cars, but many whitewashed hovels lining the road.

The Himalaya Hotel was a typical Chinese concrete block monstrosity. The temperature was plus 6 degrees Celsius, and there was no heat. Nor was there hot water until after 9:30 at night. The receptionists wore puffy down jackets to keep warm. This was ominous. We realized that we had arrived in the off-season. To add to the depressing atmosphere, fluorescent bars above us cast a blue light, making us all look pallid and ill.

We immediately headed for the Tibetan sector of town and the Barkor, where crowds of people were circumambulating clockwise, spinning their prayer wheels and saying prayers. Some astonishing women from Kham and Amdo dazzled our eyes with their braids entwined with turquoise and fastened with silver clasps. The ruddy-faced men sported fur-lined hats and sheepskin coats. They were all striking in their beauty.

We were swept along, past stalls selling prayer flags and drums, juniper and herbs, butter for lamps and all sorts of religious objects. In front of the Jokhang temple, huge mud-dried urns burned incense, thrown in by pilgrims for good merit. Deafening music blared over the square, and surveillance cameras anchored to walls recorded every movement.

> WHEN THE IRON BIRD FLIES AND HORSES RUN ON WHEELS THE TIBETAN PEOPLE WILL BE SCATTERED LIKE ANTS ACROSS THE WORLD AND THE DHARMA WILL COME TO THE LAND OF THE REDMAN.

Local monasteries were educational but empty. Where once there were 10,000 monks at Drepung, now there were only 400, and they were made to sit for indoctrination sessions every day. We were told that Tibetans are paid only a quarter of the wages of the Chinese. They were not free to travel. The monasteries had been repaired only because of the tourists.

Still, the Tibetan spirit was unbowed. Like a spring, the more it is pushed down, the more it resists. There were so many iconic images in this part of the world. The long braids on a young Tibetan girl, silver boxes at her waist, pilgrims whirling prayer drums and repeating mantras as they circled the Jokhang temple, the new leaf green of the willow trees against the cerulean blue of the sky, all these and more were etched in my mind.

I was so moved by a flood of images, I wrote a haiku poem to myself:
Enveloped by dust
The cart man pulls up his horse.
I have a sore throat.

> SHOULD YOU PLEASE CHOOSE THESE TWO SAFE EXIT IF HAPPEN SOME EMERGENCY THING AND DON'T TERRIFY ANYWAY
>
> *- Hotel fire exit sign.*

We drove all day over two high passes decorated with prayer flags and stopped to pick up a nun who had been rowed across a turquoise lake in a yak-skin boat. Sharing our lunch with her, we gave her all our extra clothes and a forbidden picture of the Dalai Lama from our guidebook. With a sharp intake of breath, she held the picture over her head and burst into tears. We all cried. The Chinese had forbidden images of this great man to punish the devoted Tibetans, and perhaps in hope that they might forget him. She left us a bit further along the road and slowly disappeared into the dry hills, returning to her monastery.

Electrical poles lined the road, not for the people, but to extract metal from the hills. Chinese military posts marked where soldiers, who doubled as miners, lived.

Our hotel in Gyantse was another concrete horror. On the door in my room was a map of the fire escape route with the following words: *Should you please choose these two safe exit if happen some emergency thing and don't terrify anyway.*

The Gyantse Kumbum was worth the entire trip to Tibet. The paintings dated to the 14th century and were reminiscent of the Italian frescoes of Giotto in their simplicity. Wind-horse prayer papers littered the floors in the chapels. A labyrinth of staircases led to the roof from which we could see a fort high on a hill. It had been fought over by the British in 1904. How remote this area must have been then.

Gyantse Kumbum

Shigatse was our next stop with its inevitable cookie-cutter hotel. Here, at Tashilhumpo Monastery we marvelled at the 26-metre-high seated Maitreya Buddha covered in gold and encrusted with pearls, diamonds, and amber. This is the home of the Panchen Lama, and I was thrilled to be seeing all this with my own eyes. How much longer would we be able to come to Tibet? There are pictures of the new Panchen Lama, chosen by the Chinese, with phony offerings around it. The people don't believe the Chinese at all.

Back in Lhasa we toured the Norbulinka, the Dalai Lama's summer home. I pocketed a leaf from a tree in the garden and saw the quarters from which he left to escape the Chinese in 1959. The guards were Tibetan communists. I gave them cold stares but, as I was learning, this only produced bad karma for me. I bought a low lama table from a family as I sat in their sunny living room and gazed out their window at the snowy mountains beyond the spare yellow-leafed poplars. Life here is hard. It was a challenge for them to preserve their own culture. They were fighting to retain their spirit against formidable odds.

On our flight over the mountains back to Nepal, the dun colours of the high plateau shifted abruptly to green. I thought of the richness of Nepalese culture, the chaos and clash of colours, crowds and religions. Returning to Kathmandu was like arriving in New York after the emptiness and barrenness of Tibet.

chapter 10

TEA WITH KING OF MUSTANG

1995 | GORD

The route to Mustang

Mustang (pronounced Moose-tang) is located in central Nepal and is an extension of the Tibetan plateau. It is referred to as a wing of the roof of the world. At an elevation above 3,700 metres, the air is both thin and dry. Mustang lies in the rain shadow of the Annapurna range, and moisture is fleeting at the best of times. The 6,000 locals live on animal husbandry, tourism, and sporadic trade between Tibet and India. The horse rules here – it is the only means of transportation in the kingdom. Personal wealth is measured in the number of horses a farmer owns.

But all this will change soon with the prospect of a road that will bisect Mustang within the next 20 years joining Nepal and Tibet. It was our good fortune to be there before this culture disappears.

The region has been ruled by a king since the Middle Ages and was unknown to the outside world until the mid-20th century. The brutal occupation of Tibet by the Chinese in 1959 brought Mustang into the world news. The Khampas, who were the last Tibetans to hold out against the Chinese, used Mustang as their final bastion of resistance. They were eventually defeated with the aid of the Nepali government.

In its heyday, under the Mustang kings of the 15th and 16th centuries, the capital Lo Manthang was the centre of a lucrative salt-trading route. Tibetans took salt and wool south to exchange for grain from India.In the mid-19th-century, Mustang was incorporated into the newly formed country of Nepal. This trade came to a virtual halt following the invasion of Tibet by the Chinese.

It wasn't until 1952 that the first Western explorer, Michel Peissel, set foot in Mustang. Returning in 1964, he travelled extensively through the region studying the culture. His book *Travels in Mustang* was a sensation and led to the permission of limited travel to the area. Because of the lack of tourist facilities

Lo Manthang and the King's palace

and the fragile condition of historic artifacts, tourism has been kept to a minimum.

With the overthrow of the Nepal monarchy in 2008, the current King Jigmy Basta's authority had been reduced to that of an administrator.

Our Everest Trekking groups travelled from Kathmandu by Russian helicopter in October 1995. We arrived in the village of Jomson at 2,700 metres near the southern border of Mustang. Our support staff of cooks and Sherpas and the ponies that were to carry all our food and camping gear for the next two weeks were there to greet us. The team was made up of nine mules bearing duffle bags, and two "hospital" horses for anyone too sick to walk. We also had the help of nine Nepalese, which included our sirdar, and a Nepalese liaison officer.

We made an early departure to get a head start on the major thermal winds that spring up at midday. As the sun warms the desert landscape, the still mountain air is pulled to higher elevations. By early afternoon, great plumes of dust blast the mountains and everything in its way. Face scarves are a daily ritual in Mustang.

Over millennia the wind has sculpted the canyon walls into surreal shapes like organ pipes, fluted pillars, and rocky spires. High overhead, golden eagles soared in the crystal clear air. The cliffs facing the village of Chhuksang were dotted with caves, the living quarters of early inhabitants of the area, dating back to 800 BC. Later, the caves became the quarters of meditating monks.

Moving up the Kali Gandaki valley, we passed through the Tibetan-style villages of Kagbeni, Tangbe, and Chhuksang. We soon realized that we were at altitude as we started up the challenging "Golden

Staircase", a tough uphill path carved from the side of a gorge. At the top, we reached the start of the high and dusty plateau of Mustang. We camped by an oasis of poplar trees near the village of Samar with a view of the sunset over the distant massive Annapurna range. Below, the barren beauty of desert hills merged into the gathering dusk.

The following day we pitched our tents on the roof of a house at Tsarang, owned by the King's nephew, Tsewang Bista. He gave us our first understanding of how quickly life was changing in Mustang. The prospect of a road across the kingdom would spell the end of this distinct way of life.

Late on our fourth day of trekking, we crested a hill to see in the distance the walled town of Lo Manthang. Built in the 14th century, it has remained with few structural changes. Its population of 900 lived in no more than 200 houses, none higher than the royal palace. Animals lived on the ground floor, providing a semblance of heat for the people above. On the roof, brushwood and yak dung were stored. Above the entrance door was a decorative arrangement of sheep's horns, symbolic of health and prosperity. The soft, rusty oranges of the town buildings contrasted with the browns of the surrounding hills. Rounding a corner, one might have encountered a cow or horse, a flock of goats, or children playing with a homemade ball in the dusty soil.

> REMOTE, MYSTERIOUS AND ROMANTIC, LO MANTHANG DEFINED THE WORD EXOTIC.

Michel Peissel described Lo Manthang as, "the mythical fortress of a lost planet; in a lunar landscape of barren crests with jagged contours...a fortified town, whose rectangular bastion enclosed in its shelter a whole city."

We had hoped to meet King Jigme Palbar Bista, and learned that he was planning to leave at six o'clock the following morning. It was a now-or-never opportunity, so with ceremonial khata scarves we hurried to the palace. We were ushered into a meeting room, served Tibetan tea by the queen's niece, and talked to the king through our interpreter, Tashi Sherpa. The audience was a surprisingly casual affair. Dignified and relaxed, he sat in a Tibetan-style tea-room with low carpeted seating, one hand fingering prayer beads, the other stroking his Lhasa Apso dog. King Bista, who was in his 60's, was the twenty-fourth monarch in a line that stretched back to the 14th century. He presided over disputes involving water and grazing rights, inheritance questions, and cases of petty crime.

He blessed our khata scarves and placed them around our necks as a farewell gesture. The next day, we lingered on Dhali La ridge to gaze at the now-distant walls of Lo Manthang. It resembled an image of Shangri-la – the fluttering prayer flags, the vastness, the stillness. Then, like the fabled realm, it slipped from view, and we were on the trail home.

The Village of Tsarang

chapter 11

KOPAN OMS AND COPRA RIDGE

1996 | GAIL

Kopan Monastery was a highly anticipated experience for both of us. We planned to allow two days before the arrival of our group. This time to pause and reflect in silence, while only for such a short time, would point to the benefits of meditation. A Dharma talk, or instruction, would be offered each afternoon.

We had both grown up thinking that Buddhism was a faraway "religion" where people different from us worshipped graven images. Now we were aware that over 300 million people practiced this form of spiritual awakening, and our ignorance of this religion and philosophy was deplorable. Words like meditation, dharma and karma, nirvana, and noble truths were new to us. The thought that all the world's phenomena and ideas are impermanent, like a water bubble, dew, or lightning in a summer storm was foreign to our western ways.

High on a hill above the Kathmandu valley, we were assigned separate rooms – women in lower units, and men above. Our first instruction at the Dharma talk was to learn the hypnotic chant *Om Ah Hum Vajra Guru Padma Siddi Hum*, the mantra of all Buddha masters and realized beings. There are layers of meanings to these words – twelve syllables carrying twelve blessings.

On our first night, a storm gathered in the east, sending flashes of lightning across the valley. Chants rose from the main temple room, and we were drawn to the worship of a few hundred monks. A young monk, not more than ten, tumbled into sleep, to be prodded awake by the monitor. It was far past his bedtime. The scent of butter lamps and incense made me sleepy too. Later we climbed to the flat roof where the only object was a small glass house on a wooden table. Dozens of yak butter lamps glowed through the panes. We watched the sky while the storm passed, and the stars hung in the infinite space above. The peace of the setting, the absence of chatter and the sound of my heartbeat filled me with a sense of completeness and oneness with my surroundings.

The next morning a horn practice on the hill above our rooms filled the morning air with deep resonant sounds. The setting was spectacular. Crows cawed, birds sang, and I couldn't imagine being in a place more filled with peace.

We met our group and flew to Pokhara. Shortly after landing we noticed a group of Australians throwing pens and gum at a group of children. "This is what they want," they said, "and we're gonna give it to them." Many tourists don't understand that this teaches children to beg. Often the people in poorer countries look at tourists as walking moneybags and gift givers because many tourists feel guilty about the difference between all they have and the physical poverty of the local people. Some Nepalis feel sorry for them, feeling that they must be spiritually impoverished. We have seen children push people over, pull their clothes, and throw things at them in places where tourists misbehave by handing them money or pens or worse still, candy and sweets that destroy their teeth.

We always tell our groups to give to NGOs in the country, or SEVA, which provides the gift of sight, or to schools, but not directly to children. In 1989 I remember a child playing with a kite we had given him while we had lunch. His father made him return it to us and said he did not want his child to become a beggar.

Our destination was Copra Ridge. The weather was variable with a continual swirl of clouds, now descending, but occasionally rising to reveal spectacular peaks. Machhupuchhare mysteriously appeared in the east and dominated the landscape for two days.

By the time we reached Copra Ridge, a steady rain made the climb treacherous. I had been sick with a chest infection and fever, and this, combined with fog and mud, depressed my spirits immeasurably. The weather did not break, and the following day we huddled in the dining tent for the day playing Hearts, setting an all-time record of 36 consecutive games.

As we were unable to climb to the sacred lake, we had no choice but to descend. After our Kopan Monastery experience, I recognized the feeling of grasping and aversion, dreading the cold of night, and clinging to the sun's warmth and the promise of better health. I was happy to descend out of the pain and suffering of the cold and rain to find pleasure in warmth and a hot shower. The conscious mind was an important first step for me to recognize being in the moment and how all was changing.

chapter 12

SOLU

OUR BODIES SAID STOP BUT OUR
SPIRITS SAID NEVER

1998 | GAIL

A group of guys who played hockey together in an "old timers" league decided to come to Nepal with some of their wives and a couple of friends. They were wildly enthusiastic about being together on this adventure to the point that one man, Bill, said nothing about having pneumonia prior to leaving. He had checked himself out of the hospital early and, still on Demerol, backed his car into a tree. This resulted in a sore back, which added to his medical woes. Bill was not going to miss this trip! An arthritic hip and some plantar fasciitis were among ailments others failed to mention.

Because many of the men ran their own companies, they had made a pact before they left Canada to try hard not to be bossy. When one of them seemed to want to take charge, the others all together chanted, "baaa." They were to be sheep and follow directions. So on day one, when the Sherpas were putting up our tents, Larry said, "Why the hell are they putting the tents over there?" "Baaa" was the chant from the men used to being in charge, and then he remembered: "Ahh yes!"

That same day the guys thought it would be fun to carve walking sticks, and one of them cut his thumb severely. Fortunately Nola, a nurse, Steri-Stripped and bandaged the wound immediately and professionally so infection never set in.

On this trip we gave money to the Ringmu School as we passed through, and continued up to and over the Taksingdu La. The eponymous monastery nearby was in disrepair although a few monks still lived there.

The next day we walked across the valley to Kalden Sherpa's family farmhouse at Solung. At the time, Kalden drove the little ferryboat around False Creek in Vancouver. Tourists asked him if he was First Nations, and he often answered positively just for fun. Before we left, he had given us gifts of socks and money for his father. We met his parents, and a couple of us had a snooze on the straw in their sunny farmyard. This was a big mistake, as that act precipitated a week of itching bug bites and red welts wherever our bodies had touched the straw.

We visited the famous Thubten Choling monastery where Ang Nuri, our sirdar, and I received a blessing from the abbot. Trulshik Rinpoche settled here after fleeing Tibet in 1959. He had thought he would return, but that was not to be, and at this time there were over 900 monks and nuns settled along this north Solu mountain slope. Ang Nuri's mother was a nun here because her duties in Ringmu had come to an end, and this was where she wanted to live out her days.

Ang Nuri had seven children and three were attending boarding school at Phugmoche, built on a huge rock above Tubten Choling at 3,100 metres. He paid $125 a year each for this privilege. Seventy children had full room, board, and schooling there.

The hockey guys were far more interested in a small 30,000-watt electrical plant by a river than the religious side of life there, and all wanted to pin down their exact altitude on their altimeters several times a day. This seemed to me to be a male preoccupation.

It was cloudy and increasingly cold, and the guys played cards every night. There was no chance to wash clothes as we were heading into colder mountain weather on Mt. Peekay.

It snowed the night before our climb. Breakfast at five was rice porridge and eggs, and soon we were tramping up a steep path through a light dusting of snow among stunted rhododendron trees. The air was thin, and I had to sit down after every 30 steps. I had a headache, but after a couple of hours of mumbling one of my mantras, "This-is-so-good," I arrived at the top with the rest of them. The view with the clear blue sky was staggering. From Kanchenjunga to Langtang, we saw all the major peaks including Everest.

A 1,200-metre descent took us down the Loding Valley to warmth and a night in a lovely meadow. At breakfast the next morning, we looked far up the hills to what was now our mountain.

Bill's shirt was printed with block letters: Our bodies said STOP but our spirits cried NEVER! Dave made the comment of the trip: "Two more nights in a f***ing tent!" He had run out of cigarettes and was desperate to get to more.

Our porters had been carrying one and a half loads because this was a relatively short trip. This meant 45 to 50 kilos or about 100 pounds. Many of them had just finished carrying 80 kilos from Jiri to Namche Bazar, a distance of nine days' walking. After lunch one day, John asked to try to carry one of the porter's loads. The tumpline was placed over his forehead and three men pushed him up to a standing position. A short wobble and he was slammed to the ground. The small porter laughed, picked up the 50-kilo load, and trotted off down the trail. Larry's comment as an old hockey player was, "Yeah...but can he play defense?"

On our last night in the hotel in Phaplu, tips were distributed, and the porters were given a party for 600 rupees – about $15. We all danced together until 10:00 p.m., at which point the porters were staggering drunk and the party ended. The hotel was full to overflowing. Many local people were there for Mani Rimdu, the full moon festival in the area. This is a time when traditional stories are told in dance at Chiwong Monastery, and Buddhist cultural history is celebrated.

The hockey guys thought that all the monks and their followers were people having some kind of mid-life crisis.

We left by Russian helicopter the next morning, shopped in Kathmandu, and flew down to the south of the country for a jungle experience at the famous Tiger Tops Lodge. There we watched elephant polo on the airstrip and rode the beasts to look for tiger, rhinos, monkeys, and deer.

The hockey guys racked up a monster bar bill, and we flew back to Kathmandu.

Just before the final dinner, Bill found himself in great pain with cramps in his legs. He and I went to Emergency at the Patan Hospital, where we lined up with crowds of people to register. There was one person behind a wicket at the end of the room. Being tourists, we had preferential treatment and were able to see a Western doctor. He was unconcerned about the cramps, but far more worried about the fluid in Bill's lungs. It now appeared that Bill had done the entire trek with low-grade pneumonia. The cramps disappeared, fortunately, and later he was able to come to our final dinner.

We arrived back in Canada and lined up to grab our bags. Dave, a lawyer, was ushered into a special room at customs because a sniffer dog smelled something suspicious in his Everest Trekking bag. When they opened the bag, customs officials recoiled at the odour emanating from three weeks of unwashed and very stinky clothes.

With fluid still in his lungs, Bill hugged his loving wife, cramps gone, guitar in hand, and a smile on his face. Pride, courage, admiration, and stubbornness were elements dominating the group dynamics on this trip.

ABREAST IN A BOAT TO ABREAST IN NEPAL

1999 | GAIL

We came from Winnipeg, Portland, Victoria, and Vancouver. Our average age was 54. What we had in common was breast cancer – and paddling. We were all members of dragon boat teams, raising awareness that there is life and adventure after breast cancer. We were setting out half way around the world to prove it "big time" and climb a mountain in Nepal.

Morning dawned clear and cold, and after a hearty breakfast, we hiked up through stunted rhododendron forests on a steep stony path. The air was thin, and a dusting of snow made the trail challenging.

This was the big day. We were climbing Peekay, a 4,100 metre mountain. On the summit we would be higher than the tops of most of Canada's mountains.

The night before, as yaks grazed near our tents, the clouds had rolled in. We'd warmed our hands on hot soup cups at dinner while wind whipped the loose flaps on the sides of our dining tent, making the lantern swing perilously. Rain formed rivulets in the canvas roof and dripped onto our table. Our apprehension was palpable.

"If the weather is bad in the morning, we can always descend," I ventured.

Sandi mumbled, "This isn't trekking, it's bloody mountain climbing."

Laurie grumbled, "This is not my agenda. I don't have to get to the top."

Just a few days before, we had witnessed some of the Mani Rimdu ceremony at Chiwong Monastery. When the autumn moon is full, the monks dance in a timeless and obscure ritual of swirls, masks, and tassels. The head monk, or Rinpoche Trulshig, which means "Precious Destroyer of Illusion", presided over the festival. He had arrived by horse from his monastery on the other side of the valley.

ALL OF US WERE REACHING FAR
AND DIGGING DEEP.

There was no question that this man had an aura of peace and calm about him. We were fortunate to be blessed by him. We brought a lock of hair from one of our paddling friends who was suffering

from chemotherapy and the spread of her disease. In a moving moment he took the lock and blessed it especially for us while a crowd of a hundred waited for their turn. We took the lock up to the high mountains where it remains in the cairn on top of Peekay, radiating its blessings on Jane, who is still vibrantly and happily with us.

In paddling terms all of us were reaching far and digging deep. Slowly apprehension dissolved into determination. This was familiar ground. We had drawn on inner resources to overcome self-doubt before. Having dealt with breast cancer, we paddlers knew we could handle just about any challenge. Our fellow trekkers quickly felt the same way.

Empowered by these thoughts and armed with determination, we all made it to the top of the mountain that glorious day. The scenery was stunning. We could see the snowy peaks of the Himalaya from Kanchenjunga to Annapurna. Set like a jewel in the centre was Everest. There were hugs and congratulations. We unfurled our "Abreast in a Boat" flag to display before the world's highest mountain in exuberant appreciation for our paddling sponsors. The Sherpas strung prayer flags on poles. Found in a local market, the flags had been blessed by the high Lama at Chiwong Monastery and were now offered to the winds, fluttering their mantra *Om Mani Padme Hum*, Praise to the Jewel in the Heart of the Lotus.

On this adventure, the challenge was embraced with enthusiastic strength and courage, and the rewards were immeasurable.

A HOLY LAKE AND A BUDDHIST FESTIVAL

2012 | GORD

I returned to the Solu in 2012, beginning our trek at Junbesi, an old Sherpa village with a charming Gompa. With a group of ten, we began a steep climb to our first campsite above the tree line. Arriving in the late afternoon, we found our tents in place and the kitchen staff busy making dinner. The setting was a Himalayan high, 360 degrees of snow-covered mountains and billowing clouds. When a still and starlit night unfolded, the temperature dipped into the freezing range.

The next day we followed an undulating grassy ridge to reach our campsite at Beni at 4,100 metres, a cold and inhospitable plateau at the base of the Numbur glacier. This was our launch position for the 400-metre climb to Dudh Kunda. The sun disappeared mid-afternoon, and immediately the temperature dropped below freezing. Unusually high humidity caused frost to accumulate on the tent roof panels, telling us it was to be a cold night. Even the prospect of a rousing game of Hearts could not persuade the group to postpone the pleasure of their sleeping bags. A winter scene greeted us in the morning with heavy frost everywhere. Soon the sun filled the valley, and we were again blessed with the prospect of a fine day of climbing to our destination.

Dudh Kunda is a holy lake surrounded by glaciers at the base of Mt. Numbur. Each August, thousands of pilgrims climb here to be blessed by its sacred water. Makeshift stone structures provide shelter for both Hindu and Buddhist devotees. Offerings of coins, clothes, and prayer flags are found along the edge of the lake. It is such an inspiring place that my nephew Doug brought his brother's ashes, and in a solitary moment released them to become one with the surroundings.

We descended 1,400 metres to the Taksingdu La over the following two days to the grounds of a

Buddhist monastery. The air was rich with oxygen, and flowers decorated window boxes. Clothes were hung to dry. It was time to lie in the sun and plan for the trip ahead to the Chiwong Gompa, where we were to witness the ancient Buddhist dances held in the courtyard of the monastery for the local Sherpa population – and a few lucky foreigners.

Prior to the performances we were offered an audience with the Rinpoche Sang Sang in an upper chamber of the monastery. We entered his small room through a curtain. Morning sunshine poured through a window on our right. In his traditional maroon robes Rinpoche sat before us in the lotus position and gestured to us to enter. Bearing khata scarves, we received a warm and friendly welcome. Our scarves were presented, blessed, and placed around our necks.

Mani Rimdu embodies the prayers of Chenrezig, the god of compassion. Each monastery has its own style of dancing, performed on the last two days of the seventeen-day puja or ritual worship. People come for the blessing of the Rinpoche and to receive the rilbu, a pill that cures and makes the path to the after-life easier.

There are sixteen dances, each representing a puja performed during the previous days. To the drone of horns and cymbals, masked dancers swirl and sway in a mesmerizing pattern, their masks representing deities of long life and wisdom. The dances conclude with a ritual to exorcise evil.

Monks in yellow robes and curved hats sat cross-legged on the stage. The Rinpoche rested in the lotus position on a separate dais. Fabric draped over the open courtyard, shaded the dancers from the sun.

Mani Rimdu has become a popular tourist spectacle, particularly in the Khumbu, the Sherpa district that lies north of Solu. Fewer than 900 visitors come to Solu, but 25,000 tourists travel to the Khumbu for the Mani Rimdu ceremony at Tengboche Monastery. There, the campground is overcrowded, and tickets must be issued to enter the monastery building, as public space is limited. At Chiwong, the celebration was delightfully unspoiled.

chapter 13

BHUTAN

SCOUTING THE LAND OF GROSS
NATIONAL HAPPINESS

1997 | GORD

O ur plane performed hazardous acrobatics as it approached the Paro airstrip. The peaks above Bhutan's only airport are at almost 5,500 metres, and we seemed to shave the roofs of farmhouses as we slalomed through the surrounding hills. This is one of the world's most dangerous airstrips. Eyes tight shut, I prayed that our pilot knew his stuff. Only eight commercial pilots were certified to land there, and Druk Air was the only airline with access to the country. It was 1997, and Ross Macdonald and I were on a scouting tour to check out the mysteries in the "*Land of the Thunder Dragon*" and plan for future treks.

We were surprised by what we found: Paro, with a speed limit of 9 kmh (the pace of a bicycle), betel nuts that replaced tobacco, a high-quality education system, a revered Buddhist king with three wives (all sisters) and a population of only 600,000. All of this was in sharp contrast to Nepal, and its 20 million souls, political disarray, and a disinterested monarchy that had long overstayed its welcome.

In 1972, as an alternative way to measure the quality of life, King Jigme Singme Wangchuck proposed a happiness index or Gross National Happiness. Its four Buddhist tenets were defined as promoting sustainable development, preserving and promoting cultural values, conserving the natural environment, and establishing good governance. This was new to us and certainly would be interesting to others we would bring.

Tobacco sales were not allowed, mountain peaks were off-limits to climbers, forestry was strictly controlled, and the air space was limited to the national carrier Druk Air. It was mandatory for the Bhutanese to wear the national costume, the gho for men and kira for women. All travellers were met and accompanied by a guide while in the country. In 1997 the daily cost for visiting, as set by the tourism department was US $285 a day, which included hotel, meals, transportation, and a full-time Bhutanese guide.

Our ambassador was Mr. Tinley and his pristine and precious Toyota sedan. Only recently he had been a monk in a Thimphu monastery, and he took this new position with a curious level of seriousness. He seldom drove faster than 30 kmh, and should there be glass on the road, he would stop the car, cut branches to make a broom, and sweep the road clean.

AN UNEXPECTED SNOWSTORM

1999 | GORD

A group of eight from Toronto and Calgary joined me for our first Bhutan trek. Surprises were awaiting us! The perfect autumn weather ended on our second day in the country. I didn't know that a hurricane was pounding the east coast of India, and this resulted in six days of rain and snow for our trek to Chomolhari Base Camp. The gentle rain on day one persisted through to day three, and by the time we had reached an altitude of 3,500 metres, the rain had turned to snow. As we dragged ourselves into base camp, wet and cold, we passed the few remaining groups heading down. Not a good sign!

In my group was a high-powered businessman who had spent most of his life imparting knowledge and advice in the office. This was likely the first time in his adult life that he was not in control, which he found uncomfortable and difficult. As a result, he was rude and surly, and as conditions worsened, so did his behaviour. He referred to me as "KA-nance," purposely mispronouncing my name and questioning my ability as a trek leader. However, each time he stepped out of line with another rude comment, the positive and delightful women in the group became my allies and publicly scolded him. They provided an essential balance in the group that allowed us to overcome the difficult conditions that lay ahead.

After a full day of walking in rain and then snow, our arrival at Chomolhari Base Camp could not have been more depressing. The dark clouds hung low in the valley, the temperature was below freezing, and a heavy wet snow was falling. The staff struggled to set up camp, and by the time dinner was ready, we knew we were in for a cold and miserable night. By the following morning, we were in a full-blown Himalayan blizzard. Overnight, our tents had collapsed, forcing us to move into a small stone shelter for protection from the elements. We were able to build a sputtering fire to dry wet clothing. A half metre of snow fell over two days, and I was beginning to fear for our safety. Our ponies had been taken down earlier – we were on our own.

To our relief, we awoke on the third day to brilliant sunshine. We quickly packed our gear and started our descent in the knee-deep snow to dry ground eight hours away. It was slow going and soon day became night. The group had gone ahead to our tree-line campsite at Thangthanka at 3,750 metres. I stayed back with Judy, who was dealing with an injured knee. With moonlight overhead, we picked our way through a watery, muddy field, stepping from dry boulder to boulder. I was leading and calling out, "Over here, Judy. This way, Judy." Suddenly, there was a mighty splash behind me! Without comment, a soggy Judy picked herself up out of the muck, and we pressed on to arrive at a most welcome campsite. Judy received the *Perseverance Award* that evening as we reviewed the day in the dining tent.

Two days later, we were back to civilization and Paro village.

Our first stop was a small lodge, well stocked with beer. Elated to be in a room that was cozy and warm, the group spirit was electric. I was sitting on a couch next to my nemesis. With beer in hand, he put an arm around my shoulder and said, "Gord – we did it! That was the greatest trip ever!"

The next day, we had a group lunch in a Thimphu restaurant prior to our departure for home the following morning. My antagonist did not join us, but instead went shopping with our guide. Just as we finished lunch, the door opened and the strangest of figures entered the room. There he was, decked out in an upscale Bhutanese gho complete with a white scarf. This was the final act in what was later referred to as "The Metamorphosis of a Nemesis".

Tashi once said to me, "The trouble with you Westerners is you all have expectations." It was pointless to merely hope for good weather. Hoping meant nothing, and our lesson was the need to accept events as they unfolded and deal with the situation moment to moment.

GODS WIN, DEMONS LOSE

2000 | GORD

T he following year we returned to Bhutan to trek the western half of the famous Snowman Trek. Our group consisted of five British and five Canadian clients. In this country our supplies were carried on the backs of ponies rather than porters, and the staff was much smaller in number than in Nepal. Only two horsemen, two kitchen boys, and three guides were necessary for twelve trekkers.

Prior to departure, I gave my usual briefing about trek safety and staying healthy, which included the standard recommendation to avoid alcohol while trekking at altitude. At our first campsite just before dinner, I heard the voice of Roger, our British friend, booming into the night, "The bar is nooww OPEN!" He proceeded over the following two weeks to disprove the fact that alcohol and altitude do not mix. He and his British cohort had strong constitutions and a penchant for ritual!

Ken of Vancouver had been with me in Nepal a few years earlier. He was a well-travelled Buddhist doctor. Although we had supplied sleeping bags in Nepal, they were not on our list in Bhutan, and he missed that message before our two-week remote high-altitude trek. It wasn't until late in the first day as we followed the laden ponies along the trail that he realized his mistake. Ken sidled up to me and sheepishly proclaimed, "Gord, bad news. I don't have a sleeping bag." Fortunately, I had an extra summer weight bag with me. One of the guides kindly split his double sleeping bag, and for the next fourteen nights, Ken piled on five layers of clothes before bedtime and slept in frigid conditions without complaint.

This was a two-week hike from Paro to Chomolhari Base Camp and east along the Tibetan border to Laya. We hiked by the tiny, remote settlements of Lingshi, Chebisa, and Limithang, where farmers were harvesting barley by hand. For ten days we crossed passes in excess of 5,000 metres, until we reached the remote village of Laya. Here we rested in this timeless land on the Tibetan border where the women wore conical bamboo hats and dressed in colourful kiras, the national dress.

Following a day of rest, we left Laya and turned south to descend along a river gorge through dense forests carpeted with a profusion of rare and endangered flowers. Neilly, a British botanist and photographer, was collecting seeds for Kew Gardens near London. Bhutan is one of the ten top countries for biological diversity in the world. There are over fifty species of rhododendrons.

This two-week trek ranked as one of our most outstanding Himalayan experiences. It was exotic and remote. We passed through medieval villages untouched by modern conveniences. The autumn weather was unusually stable, and we were able to traverse five high mountain passes just ahead of the winter snow. As we climbed each pass, we synchronized our footsteps with our breath, one step with the in-breath and the next with the out-breath. Approaching the tops of the passes, ubiquitous stone markers indicated the end of the long slog up. The wind was often fierce, and we would pause for just a moment to catch our breath and call, *Lha Gey Lo*, a traditional blessing in this country. We would add a stone to the cairn and begin our descent down the other side, delighted that our call meant, "Praise to the gods of the pass." Gods win, Demons lose!

There was always a shelter out of the wind on the down side where we would have our hot lunch which had been prepared at breakfast and carried in thermos containers. After lunch and a rest, we would float down to a narrow valley, and I don't think I have ever felt so in harmony with my body. I could actually feel new energy coursing through my veins to the tips of my fingers and toes.

GANGKAR PUNSUM – AS REMOTE AS IT GETS

2009 | GORD

In 2009 we organized a trek to the base camp of Bhutan's highest peak, Gangkar Punsum, located in central Bhutan north of the Bumthang district. Our group of three Brits and five Canadians met at the Paro airport in mid-October to make the two-day drive east to Jakar, the capital of the province. Approximately 200 people completed this high trek each year. We were fortunate that we saw few trekkers, and that we had unusually clear weather.

Base Camp at 4,600 metres was on a plain at the end of which rose the dramatic face of Gangkar Punsum at 6,800 metres. This was the highest unclimbed massif in the world. Our tent doors faced the mountain, and when we awoke to the delightfully accented words, "Tea, sir," the peak was bathed in the gold of the rising sun. Minus 12 degrees Celsius would not inhibit the start of another grand day in the Himalaya. Six days later, this valley would be covered with a metre of snow.

Our return route was to have taken us over the Thole La, but due to altitude sickness in our group, we elected to retrace our steps and follow the rushing waters of the Chamkhar Chhu back to Tocktu Zampa. Within two days, the rich air brought relief to those feeling the effects of altitude at base camp.

We came upon teams of men dressed in gohs and carrying bows and arrows. It was a village archery contest, the national sport of Bhutan. Each archer carried two arrows. Staring down the 140 metre range, we strained to focus on the small wooden target propped up on the dusty ground. When an arrow struck, team members darted out from behind a protective wall, linked arms, and hopped from one foot to the other in a celebratory dance. There were cheerers and jeerers on the sidelines, all dressed in traditional garb, offering tea, chanting, dancing, drinking, and serving ara, an alcoholic drink made from millet or rice. The festive atmosphere might go on for days at a time, as the contests are known to be slow. In earlier times, a contest could be a month long.

On our return to Jakar, we were treated to the Jampey Lhakang Drup, one of the most spectacular of all Tsechus in Bhutan. A Tsechu is a Buddhist dance festival to honour Guru Rinpoche, the Tibetan saint who brought Buddhism to the country. Local villagers gathered in a spirit of festivity, celebration, and deep faith to witness unique masked dances and celebrations. The festival began with a fire blessing ceremony; a large gate was set alight, and people passed under it to receive their blessing.

Besides the usual Bhutanese festival routine, which involved religious masked dances and folk dancing or singing, Jambay Lhakhang Drup was known for one unique event. Close to midnight, naked dances were held in a closed courtyard. A group of men swirled and twirled to the drums and cymbals, wearing only a white cloth to cover their faces. They danced outrageously to distract devils from causing havoc and misery. Photography was not allowed.

The monastery was built in 659 AD. At the entrance to the courtyard were four large prayer wheels. A number of buildings had been added over the centuries, all with golden roofs and stucco walls. Small stone chortens, built to the memory of famous lamas, were scattered about the grounds.

Dancers wore wooden or papier-mâché masks, colourfully painted and richly decorated. Performed by monks and laymen alike, the dances and sacred storytelling attracted hundreds of enthusiasts. People believed that by watching these dances, they could purify their souls and bring themselves good luck. The dancing continued for several days and included both serious and humorous stories. Jesters wearing burlesque masks goaded the bystanders with pranks, resulting in wild laughter. At the completion of the festival, the masks were returned to the temple until the following year.

To conclude our journey we visited Taktsang (Tiger's Nest) Monastery near Paro, the iconic image of Bhutan. It is believed that in the 8th century, Guru Rinpoche flew here on the back of a tiger and stayed in a nearby cave to meditate. The 17th-century structure appeared to hang from the side of the mountain with no visible access from the steep path that climbed 600 metres from the valley. Following a severe fire in 1998, the monastery was rebuilt and reopened to the general public.

Gangkar Punsum base camp 4,600 metres

chapter 14

KHUMBU COUGHS AND THE RENJO LA

2005 | GORD

Eleven hardy men and two brave women stepped onto the tarmac at the Kathmandu airport in late October 2005 for the 50-minute flight to Lukla. This was the twenty-eighth group that I had been privileged to lead into the high and exciting Himalaya.

This unique group was made up of four past trek leaders, Gary and Merv from Winnipeg, Ross from Calgary, and me. Don, our son, joined me for his first Nepal experience making the trek even more special. George and David his brother-in-law and Andreas came from Vancouver and Leney and Jim from Winnipeg chose to cross the Renjo La as an extension of their honeymoon. To complete the group, Judy, our popular leader and her son, Brian, joined us from Oakville. Tashi, our partner and long-time friend in Kathmandu could not resist leading us through his mountain homeland. There had been some idle talk in Vancouver about this being my last trek. After all, I was getting a little long in the tooth. While this strange rumour did not come from me, it had an element of marketing power. I could not have been more pleased with the group that came together.

Until recently the Renjo La at 5,147 metres had been closed, due to the politically sensitive valley of Bhote Kosi. At the head of the valley, the Nangpa La was the main escape route for Tibetan refugees fleeing their Chinese occupiers.

We flew to Lukla and walked to Namche Bazar with a mass of other trekkers, mostly from Europe and Japan. After two days in Namche to acclimatize, we left the crowds to climb up the valley to Thame at 3,800 metres. George and David remained in Namche Bazar with flu-like symptoms.

The Bhote Kosi valley is uninhabited above Thame, and we soon discovered the reason for this. The high and dry Tibetan plateau heats up during the day, sucking dense cool air from the lower Nepali

Khumbu region and creating extremely windy conditions. Coupled with low nighttime temperatures, these conditions made for rigorous camping.

The trek route crossed the lower end of the boulder-strewn Nangpa glacier. Here the trail became precarious for trekkers and porters. It took us an hour and a half, hopping from boulder to boulder to cross the moraine and the only campsite we could find was exposed to the elements. An afternoon exploratory trip towards the pass and the Tibetan border revealed gorgeous views of the western flank of Cho Oyu, the sixth-highest mountain in the world. This was our reward.

On our return, dinner was served at 6:30. With the temperature in the dining tent reading –11 degrees Celsius, and the wind blowing hard, we were in for a cold night! Our diminished group of nine crowded into the dining tent wearing all the clothes in their bags. I looked across the table to Leney and barely recognized her. Her down jacket was zipped up to her chin, and her head was buried in a woolly balaclava with only her eyes showing. The condensation created by people's breath filled the tent. Cards were not on the program for after-dinner entertainment, and that night the thermometer plunged to a bone-chilling -16 degrees Celsius.

The following morning, Leney, Jim, and Andreas, suffering from altitude and colds, left camp to return to Namche to be with Judy and her son, who had initially elected to stay back. The remaining six of us descended to a lower campsite in preparation to cross the Renjo La the following morning. There were more casualties, and for the first time, I was one of them, waking to bronchitis. Merv was sick with the "Khumbu cough" so we had no choice but to descend. That left Don, Ross, David, and Gary to cross the pass to the Gokyo valley along with Tashi and the crew.

Our original group of eleven was now split into four: Jim, Leney, Judy, Brian, and Andreas were on their way to Tengboche Monastery; George and David (now recovered) were climbing to Gokyo, and there they would meet up with the healthy four on the other side of the pass; and Merv and I were heading down to sick bay in a lodge in Thame and the care of Dr. Kami Sherpa. Who would have thought our merry group could become so scattered over a fourteen-day trek?

Don set a new standard for trek footwear in the Himalaya: golf shoes. The shoes gave him the comfort and traction he needed at lower elevation. It was not until he reached the rough terrain of the high pass that he switched to his trekking boots.

We passed many trekkers on the lower trails leading up to Namche Bazar. The Khumbu was reaping the benefit of the restrictive Maoist actions in the Annapurnas and other major trek areas. Many new lodges had been built there, particularly between Lukla and Namche Bazar. Comfortable lodges are now available for trekking throughout the Khumbu, and the romance and privacy of tent travel is on the wane.

The Lukla airstrip (700 metres in length) had just been paved. Canadian Twin Otter and German Dornier aircraft arrived at first light in waves of four, bringing even more trekkers into the area. Their turnaround time was five minutes. The terminal operated like a Swiss watch!

Back in Kathmandu, we luxuriated in our "home-away-from-home" – the Kathmandu Guest House and the outstanding hospitality of Rajan Sakya, Uttam Phuyal and staff.

Tourism was down that year, the stores less crowded, and the streets of Thamel not full. There was a temporary peace in Nepal, but the discussions between the Maoists and the government were so far apart that it was hard to imagine a solution. However, the country was safe for travel, even in Maoist-controlled areas such as the Annapurnas. Tourists were welcomed for their currency and charged a fee by the Maoists in all trekking areas other than the Khumbu.

We celebrated our final night with a grand dinner at the Thamel House, a menu of upscale Nepali food, raksi, and beer. There were emotional tears and many complimentary speeches. After five years away from Nepal, I felt privileged and a sense of deep pleasure to be able to return with close friends and family to the Nepali people and their beautiful country!

Gord and Don

Climbing Gokyo Ri

chapter 15

CLOSE CALL ON THE MANASLU CIRCUIT

2007 | GORD

Daramsala campsite 4,460 metres.

Our group of eight assembled in Kathmandu in late October 2007, eagerly anticipating our sixteen-day trek around the world's eighth-highest mountain, Manaslu Himal, 8,156 metres. Information about the trek route was limited to a few Internet stories, some published articles, and the odd Nepali map. We were primarily dependent on our knowledgeable Sherpa guides and the peerless Tashi Sherpa.

The mountain lies sixty kilometres east of the Annapurna range. The circuit is approached from the east and crosses four climate zones, from tropical to alpine. This trek has all the elements of the finest of Nepal, including both Hindu and Buddhist culture, protected wildlife, rhododendrons and wild flowers, raging rivers, precarious bridges, and stunning mountain scenery.

In Kathmandu we climbed into our bus and rumbled off to the trailhead, an estimated seven hours away. As we might have expected, there were to be challenges ahead. The road trip evolved into a marathon 28-hour journey over narrow mountain roads and steep terrain, culminating in an almost impassable one-lane track. By late afternoon the bus was stuck in mud, and we were left with no alternative but to camp beside the road and await rescue.

If we were to complete our circuit of Manaslu, "treading lightly" was going to be essential; that is, paying respect to local culture and patiently bending to the forces of nature. "All is changing," say the Buddhists, "and this too will change."

The following day, we could hear another bus approaching from Arughat, our destination, gears grinding and wheels spinning. We scrambled aboard, the bus lurched around and we were able to arrive at our destination. The Great Manaslu Walk was about to begin.

Soon we were forced to stop by armed Maoist cadres. Three soldiers sat at a desk decorated with red flags and demanded a "trail fee". The Maoists controlled the area of Gorkha where Manaslu was situated. It was their general practice to extort money from travellers and local businesses. Following a lengthy negotiation, we reluctantly paid them 100rs per trekker. To refuse payment would have resulted in retaliation against our staff or worse.

The circuit is 170 kilometres long, from Arughat Bazar to near Gorkha. It ends at Khudi, a village on the Annapurna Circuit. The route followed the Buri Gandaki, starting at 500 metres above sea level, and crossed the Larkya La at 5,325 metres.

During the early days of the trek we passed through a humid tropical landscape inhabited by monkeys and butterflies. The low-level Hindu villages were pleasantly natural and uncommercial. As we climbed higher out of the dark gorge the landscape opened up, and the culture subtly changed to Tibetan with richly carved mani walls, fluttering prayer flags, and the scent of burning juniper.

The trek was long and demanding. Relatively few people lived in this region, and villages were far apart. There were many suspension bridges, some of questionable safety with frayed ropes and missing planks. The monsoon had been particularly damaging to the trail, and often we, and particularly the porters, were faced with a frightening gap in the trail with nothing below but the distant river. Carrying bulky 35-kilogram loads, they had to turn sideways to jump the gap.

Larkya La 5,325 metres.

This area was restricted for trekking, and special permits were required. Only fully supported groups were permitted. Our Nepali staff consisted of four Sherpa guides, three kitchen staff, and twenty-one porters.

Meals were varied, tasty, and healthy. This was not an easy achievement in view of the spartan conditions in which the cook staff worked. Our typical day began at six, when a wake-up call with tea was followed by a pan of washing water. Breakfast was served at seven, and half an hour later we were on our way.

The weather for the ten days to the pass summit was superb – clear and sunny. Morning treks were best when the air was cool and the body felt strong. The kitchen staff would quickly walk ahead and meet us at a village teahouse with a hot lunch. By one-thirty we were back on the trail to walk for a further three to four hours. Our health blossomed. Above 3,500 metres, our pace slowed to three half days to prepare us for the thin air at the summit of the Larkya La. The change of pace allowed us to acclimatize superbly. All was going well.

The crossing of the Larkya La was the supreme challenge. Our campsite below the pass was cold and inhospitable. When the sun disappeared at four in the afternoon, the temperature plummeted below freezing and we fled to our tents and sleeping bags to keep warm. We were up at three the following morning to begin our climb to the summit. There was an air of excitement and anticipation as we moved about the campsite with headlamps in place and campfire blazing. Breakfast was shared in a dimly lit dining tent where the temperature was −6 degrees. We needed gloves to handle the cutlery.

The glow of the sunrise lifted our spirits as we climbed steadily along the moraine through barren

Horst on a horse crossing the Marsyangdi Khola

boulder fields. Soon the heat of the morning sun on our backs filled us with a sense of relief and optimism.

The crossing of the high pass had its own drama. Horst, from Kelowna, had been struggling with a foot infection, and his stomach was upset from his medication. By the time we reached the high camp, he was limping in pain, and it was questionable whether or not he would have the strength to climb higher. The thought of retracing his steps firmed his resolve to trek onward.

It was quickly evident the following morning that Horst was in trouble. The group split into two with Horst, Merv, and two Sherpas taking up the rear with me. By 11:30 we had still not reached the summit, and I decided to call for a rescue helicopter. It was not to be. Our satellite telephone was unable to connect with Tashi in Kathmandu, and as this was our only source of communication, we had no choice but to press on.

Looking back from the Larkya La the sky was clear and the wind still. It was a perfect day in the high Himalaya! We lingered at the summit, enjoying a snack, revelling in being in the moment. A column of smoke from our distant base camp at Daramsala rose vertically. Little did we know that by the next day these mountains were to be pounded by howling winds, freezing temperatures, and snow!

The descent lay before us. Beyond the pass we could see tough challenges. This was not going to be a walk in the park. Ahead of us lay twelve kilometres and a descent of 1,600 metres. The first two hours we inched over snowfields with treacherous footing. Each of us burrowed deep into our reservoirs of courage and confidence to carry on. The healthiest trekker reached camp by 4:30 p.m.; Horst, on the other hand, became weaker by the hour. He descended with arms draped over the shoulders of Rinzi

Buri Gandaki Khola

and Krishna. After seventeen hours, they arrived in camp. He had waged an epic battle, calling on all his considerable inner resources to achieve his goal with a thin smile on his face.

Horst had set an endurance record for us. In hindsight, we recognized that luck and perfect weather had played a big part in this achievement.

We still had four days of descent ahead of us on an unrelenting rough and rocky trail. A horse was found, and Horst was able to complete the trip with the sure-footed animal stepping down staircases of boulders and deftly navigating dangerous exposures.

Once down we endured one more unpleasant surprise. Another Maoist-led extortion awaited us as we drove along the gravel road. This kind of chaos and lawlessness had been prevalent since the assassination of the royal family in 2002. This time teachers, mothers, and children barred the road with rope. We paid our money and considered ourselves fortunate to leave the area.

LITTLE DID WE KNOW THAT BY THE NEXT DAY THESE MOUNTAINS WERE TO BE POUNDED BY HOWLING WINDS, FREEZING TEMPERATURES, AND SNOW!

chapter 16

SETBACKS AND SOLUTIONS

GORD

DEALING WITH ALTITUDE

Our trek program was determined by the monsoon season and phases of the moon The rainy season begins mid-May and continues through to late September. The mountains receive 80% of their moisture during that period. Streams become rivers, and valley temperatures soar into the low thirties. Travel by aircraft is restricted as all local flying is by visual flight rules only. Leeches are prevalent and prey on the warmth of the human body, silently sliding into boots and clothing. No – trekking in the monsoon season in the Himalaya is not advised. The best time to trek is in spring or fall. In the spring, the months of March and April are ideal. Days are long, nighttime freezing occurs above 4,000 metres, and flowers bloom in profusion. Rhododendron forests, which grow between three and four thousand metres, bloom in late April. Mountain slopes are ablaze with red or pink blossoms on these ancient trees. In the valley white Magnolia blooms float on their branches like butterflies.

However, the dust from the Gangetic Plain infiltrates the lower mountain valleys in early spring, and it is not until the tree line is reached that the air becomes pristine.

The summer monsoon acts like a giant washing machine, clearing the air of dust particles. As a result the months of October and November are the best times to trek. Although the days are shorter and the temperatures lower, the mountain views are spectacular. The brilliant light on snowy peaks against an ultramarine sky in clear, thin air defies description. Clouds form in the afternoon and dissipate after sunset. Nights are generally clear and reveal a star-studded sky. The phases of the moon are important. For a standard trek of 14 days, we choose the third night to coincide with the full moon. The peaks shimmer with a pale blue light and make a late night visit to the charpi (toilet) tent a near pleasure.

When trekking in the Khumbu, our second night is spent at Tashi's lodge in Namche Bazar. This gives us the opportunity for an after-dinner hike up to the helipad to see the Everest group bathed in moonlight. The prospect of stepping into the cold dark of night and climbing for twenty minutes at elevation is at first, unappealing. But once at the helipad, the view is stunningly beautiful.

To prepare clients for a trek, people are encouraged to register at least six months in advance of departure. This allows them to get fit both physically and mentally. Invariably, a last-minute registration leads to trouble on the trail; sometimes the person lacks training and is often unable to cope with cultural differences.

An information session is always held by the group leader to discuss clothing, equipment, medical issues, and training regimens. We issue duffle bags, and review daily trail routines. The most common question is, "What will be the effects of altitude?"

Everest Base Camp lies at 5,337 metres, and this is the dream destination for many trekkers. To get there, one must be prepared to deal with a number of physical challenges, the most serious of which is being able to cope with the thinning air. While symptoms of altitude mountain sickness (AMS) could occur as low as 3,000 metres, the ability to climb above an elevation of 4,500 metres without showing the effects of edema (accumulation of fluid) is the real test. We refer to this elevation as the "glass ceiling".

We discovered that one in four trekkers experiences difficulty getting above that altitude. Symptoms include loss of appetite, poor sleep, and headaches. To climb higher with these symptoms invites serious and even life-threatening problems. Medication helps, but caution has to prevail. Descent is the best solution, and just 300 metres can be sufficient to allow a trekker to rest and recover before returning to altitude.

When a client shows altitude symptoms, our leader has to act quickly with an order to descend. This is not always easy to do, for most trips to the Himalaya are "trips of a lifetime." In our experience men find it more difficult than women to accept this decision.

Our first trek in Nepal was with a large US travel company for a three-week trek to Everest Base Camp in the spring of 1987. Cyril had not had time to acclimatize and suffered from pulmonary edema. This was a sobering lesson for us. Rushing into the high country above 3,600 metres can be life-threatening.

Eleven years later I was guiding a group of four men to Everest Base Camp. All were fit and had prepared well for the trek. Our 25% rule was exceeded this time as two succumbed to altitude. Marty from Alberta began losing his appetite and energy above 3,500 metres. By Dingboche 4,200 metres, he had a splitting headache and was sleeping badly. It was time to leave. I asked him to descend, and in the morning, he was carried down 1,000 metres to Namche Bazar.

Frank had more complex physical problems. As he was moving with difficulty above Pheriche 4,300 metres, I decided that he should stay behind and spend an extra night at Lobuche 4,600 metres while the remainder of the group pressed on to climb Kala Pattar. On our return the following day, we met Frank at Lobuche and began our descent to Namche Bazar. We had walked for two hours, and as we passed through Pheriche and the medical clinic, his friend Roger asked me, to my surprise, if Frank had admitted to blacking out a number of times the previous day. I immediately stopped him, and together we returned to the altitude clinic for a medical examination. At a cost of US$30, a young volunteer doctor from Alaska examined him. It was a small, rudimentary examining room, and the doctor was dressed in a down jacket and fur boots.

I remained in the examination room to watch the doctor perform a series of tests for AMS: balance, eyes, lungs, and heart. He asked Frank to take five deep breaths. Fortunately, he was sitting in a chair as he lost consciousness on the fourth breath. Immediately, an oximeter was placed on his finger and together we watched in amazement as Frank's pulse sank from 90 to 40 in less than a minute. There it stabilized and then slowly began to return to a normal beat.

Other medical people in the clinic gathered to discuss Frank's condition and concluded that he must be evacuated immediately. A phone call to Tashi in Kathmandu resulted in our first helicopter rescue. Tashi delivered US$4,000 cash to the flight company, and within two hours Frank was picked up and flown to Kathmandu. Tashi's wife, Nancy, met the plane and took Frank to the Canadian medical clinic. He flew home to London the following day. His travel medical insurance policy covered the cost of the helicopter, and he subsequently had a pacemaker installed in his chest. We were fortunate to have been close to one of the few mountain clinics in Nepal.

I found that groups of women were easier to manage than men. Men often thought of themselves as stronger, faster, and fitter so when AMS hit, it was sometimes considered an embarrassment and ignored in the hope that it would go away. Women tended to be upfront when asked about their sleep, appetite, and general well being. When taking a male group above the glass ceiling of 4,500 metres, the leader needed to be particularly observant for AMS warning signs.

Guy from Winnipeg was the perfect male client for the Everest trek. A fit ex-hockey player, he was a delight to be with. His favourite expressions involved a hockey puck, as in "the puck has been dropped" (when we started the day's trek) or "time to drop the puck" (a steep climb ahead). He disguised his deteriorating condition as we ascended above Pheriche and did not tell me that he had been sleeping badly and his head was pounding. Our climb to Lobuche was 570 metres, and we ascended at an easy pace, reaching our lodge by three in the afternoon just as the sun was setting behind the peaks. As dramatically as the temperature dropped that day, Guy suddenly hit the floor of his room. He was felled by cerebral edema – a splitting headache and vomiting. Alerted by his roommate, we had to act fast with oxygen (standard equipment for all treks above 4,000 metres). After twenty minutes of full-volume oxygen, Guy was stabilized and sufficiently comfortable. We were able to wait until the following morning to return to Pheriche and await the group's return in two days. Guy was a chastened man with a new respect for the perils of high mountain travel.

In one of my early treks to altitude in the Khumbu, Tony and John from Ottawa were showing the classic altitude symptoms at first camp above Namche Bazar at an altitude of 3,800 metres. My mistake had been to use our rest day at Namche Bazar for an easy climb to the Everest View Hotel for the spectacular Everest panorama view, rather than allow everyone to stay in Namche Bazar. A day later, both Tony and John had joined the 25% club on arriving at camp. Their disappointment was bitter when told they must descend to Namche Bazar. This meant to them that their holiday was over.

That was another learning experience, confirming the formula for trekking above 3,000 metres. A rest day was needed every third day, at least three litres of fluid had to be consumed daily, and plenty of sleep was also important. In addition, ascent should not exceed 300 metres a day, and a rest day should be taken after each 1,000 metres of gain.

The magic of descending was that health returned quickly. Four days later, Tony and John were able to meet us below our destination of Gokyo Ri to enjoy the glory of the high Khumbu.

On a trek in 1996 to Gokyo, I faced an unusual emotional challenge. About six weeks prior to our departure, Angela, one of our group, called to say that her husband had just died suddenly and she must cancel. A few weeks later, she called to say she had changed her mind – her family had reminded her that it was his wish that she see the Himalaya.

We reached Gokyo on our eighth day and retired early to our sleeping bags to prepare for the pre-dawn ascent. As we set out before sunrise to climb the 600 metres to Gokyo Ri, I realized what a mental and physical trial this was for her. She had been carrying her husband's ashes and each day she struggled to contain her emotions while dealing with the altitude. At nine o'clock we were perched on the top of Gokyo Ri. Before us stretched the stunning peaks of the Cho Oyu, Pumori, Nuptse, Everest, and Lotse Shar.

Approaching Gorak Shep, Khumbu

Angela and I remained behind as the group began their descent. While I sat on the summit, she disappeared behind a large rock to sprinkle her husband's ashes. A few moments later, she reappeared, her grief replaced with a sense of joy and closure.

The following winter in Vancouver, we celebrated our Nepal experiences over dinner with a number of friends from various treks. Peter, an architect from West Vancouver, was one of the group. He and his wife, Brita, had been with me on Annapurna West in 1990. Peter was now a widower as Brita had died unexpectedly. Angela was one of our dinner guests. A few weeks later, unknown to us, Peter and Angela met by chance on a street in Vancouver.

The next Christmas we were invited to Peter's for dinner. His front door opened and both Peter and Angela were there to greet us. This was our first successful Everest Trekking romance!

The rewards of trekking to altitude are enormous. The clarity of the air makes distant mountains appear closer, the sky is an impossibly deep ultra-marine blue, and clouds hang on the peaks like cotton candy. The scale of the surrounding mountains in the Himalaya is stunning. Even at Everest Base Camp, the summit of Everest is a further 3,500 metres overhead. We become the size of ants. The delight in reaching these altitudes is enduring but to do so requires patience and discipline.

LOST DUFFLE BAGS – WHERE DID THEY GO?

I t's one thing to lose your baggage in a big city where there are stores within walking distance of your hotel and credit cards in your pocket. It's quite another when you are climbing to a wilderness elevation in the Himalaya, and your 15-kilo duffle bag containing your warm clothing, important accessories, and precious medical prescriptions goes missing.

We supply duffle bags to all trekkers for a few important reasons. Each trekker is limited to 15 kilos to be carried by a porter for the duration of the trek, and each porter carries two duffle bags, plus his personal belongings. It is important that the two duffle bags are similar in size and weight to simplify his load.

Secondly, the bags are a distinctive green and identified with our corporate name. As a result, they are easy to spot on airport baggage conveyors, fast to count on the back of a truck, and quick to see in a mountain village.

But while they are designed to be visible, they are not difficult to lose.

Beverly was meeting our group in Kathmandu in the spring of 2000 to trek to Everest Base Camp. She flew a circuitous route from Toronto, and on her arrival, her Everest Trekking bag was missing. Tashi followed up with the airlines over the following two days, but to no avail. On day three, we flew to Lukla to start the two-week trek without Bev's bag. Fellow trekkers and the local shops provided enough gear for her to continue the trek. She made the best of a patch-up job, and I admired her determination to do so without all her precious articles of comfort and survival. She had resigned herself to a wilderness trek with make-do gear.

Four days into the trek we arrived at our campsite at Deboche 3,700 metres. As the sun was disappearing behind the mountains and we were preparing to have tea in a lodge, I heard, "Mr. Gordon, Mr. Gordon, porter coming." I looked down the trail, and there it was – Beverly's green duffle bag on the shoulders of a porter. The reception by Beverly and the group was one of pure joy. She threw herself onto the bag and hugged it with tender affection.

We could only imagine the number of people who had handled the bag between the international airport in Kathmandu, the domestic terminal for the flight to Lukla airport, and the waiting porter who carried it for three days to our campsite at Deboche.

In the fall of 1992, Sue of Vancouver was part of a group trekking in the high Khumbu. We had landed at noon at Lukla and walked until late afternoon to our campsite at Phakding. Our destination was Gokyo, with some of the group doing an extension over the Cho La. We had an unusually large number of porters – probably 25 – who carried food, equipment, and our green duffle bags. Our campsite was behind a wall of stones, and one of the Sherpa guides was standing by the gate to make sure every porter made the turn at a small opening for the first night of camping.

Somehow, he missed the porter who was carrying Sue's duffle bag. As the tents were being assembled, tea was made for the trekkers, and it was then that Sue discovered her bag was missing. No one had seen her porter. What had happened? The Sherpas immediately re-traced our steps down the valley thinking the porter may have turned back. But there was no sign of either the porter or the bag. It was not until the next day that the mystery was solved. The porter had missed the gate, and as he had been hired to carry the bag to Namche Bazar, he didn't stop until he reached his destination the next day. Much to our relief, Sue was reunited with her bag on our arrival in Namche Bazar.

GIVING BACK - RINGMU ELEMENTARY SCHOOL

Imagine sitting on a wooden bench in a room with walls of stone and an earth floor. You are a ten-year-old son of a farmer, and you have been attending school for most of this first year. It is monsoon season, and the noise of the rain on the tin roof is deafening.

You can scarcely hear the teacher who holds a piece of chalk and writes something on the blackboard. You have a slate and a piece of chalk too. There are no pictures in the room, no books, no electricity, and it is hard to see in the dark room. Moisture is driven through the gap between the wall and the roof, and you are damp and cold. Your sister can no longer attend because someone has to care for the baby while your mother works in the fields. Anyway, what good is school if she is just going to marry and have children? You are needed to help out in the fields, so your parents can hardly see any benefit to your sitting all day with a slate and chalk.

Before 1950 the Ranas, who ruled Nepal, feared education for the masses, so the population was kept illiterate. The Gurkhas who fought for Britain in World War II returned knowing how to read and write and began to teach in the villages.

Ringmu is a village near the Taksingdu la, a pass that separates the Solu and Khumbu districts in the Everest region of Nepal.

We discovered the village school in 1994 while trekking through the upper Solu district. Gail and her "Oh My God" group of seniors from West Vancouver noticed the modest little structure at the edge of the trail, a stone's throw from the village square. Two dilapidated buildings with small doors and a few

windows piqued their curiosity. "Was this a shed for animals?" they wondered. Inside, forty children sat on wooden benches. The principal's office was a desk and a shelf, nothing more, and all this was in a district that's considered wealthy by Nepal standards.

A donation was enthusiastically collected on the spot and given to the school for supplies, and that was the beginning of our long association with education in the upper Solu.

Five teachers and a principal now teach the eighty children who live within an hour's walk from the village. The curriculum includes reading, writing, arithmetic, and English language classes. Graduates can continue studies at the Hillary school in Phaplu – a three-hour walk from Ringmu.

All groups that trek with us in the Solu visit the Ringmu School, and we are always treated to a celebration. Everyone is moved by the vast chasm between what is offered here and the privileged education of students in the West, often taken for granted. Our grandson saw pictures of the kids and classrooms and wondered where their computers were. The hole in the ground out back for a toilet was beyond his imagination. He couldn't fathom a mud floor, meagre lunch, torn sandals, or the lack of opportunity these children faced. Toothpaste and shampoo were unheard-of luxuries.

We usually visited the school in the morning. We'd be greeted by two rows of children, each holding a marigold flower. Some held white khata scarves to offer as blessings. We would be escorted to a long table with chairs and presented with flowers while a scarf was placed over each of our heads. Tea and biscuits miraculously appeared, served by parents, and the children began their song and dance program.

Since 1994 we have been able to upgrade the facilities with windows, doors, desks, floors, chairs, and supplies, as well as provide the salary for an extra teacher. This has all been done through revenue from our slide shows and the generous ongoing donations of trekkers and friends. One of our groups brought books in Nepali, which had been donated through the organization called Room to Read, and these were offered to the library for the eager children.

chapter 17

BISTARAI JA-NAY

2012 | GORD

Bistarai Ja-nay is Nepali for "walk slowly," our mantra while walking in the Himalaya. Each day our trekkers were reminded to Bistarai Ja-nay. They were encouraged to live in the here and now, to hasten slowly with the emphasis on slowly. It was not the destination, but the journey that mattered.

Many Westerners are goal-oriented and success-driven. They are accustomed to speed and to maximizing their many self-imposed tasks. The goal posts are never out of sight. The ball must be moved ahead no matter what. This mindset brought to altitude can lead to sickness and disappointment. Trekkers have been known to weep when faced with the fact that they may not reach their anticipated goal and must descend to a lower altitude to recover.

Hastening slowly, we adapt and become one with our environment, recognizing that we may have been living out patterns of behaviour on autopilot. Here, walking slowly, we awaken to the surprise of all that is hidden in plain sight. We notice the fold of a monk's robe, the sound of our heartbeat, the sharp spikes of juniper needles surrounding inky blue berries. We try to define the colour of a butterfly and ponder the smooth skin on a porter's cheek.

On a trip to Solu in 2010, we travelled with a group from Vancouver – high powered, with a soaring energy level and very high expectations. This group wanted and expected, among other criteria, to cover ground energetically and get lots of exercise. The elements conspired against them.

We arrived at the domestic airport in Kathmandu in eager anticipation. Our porters, Sherpas, kitchen staff, and supplies were all awaiting us in Phaplu, a 40-minute flight away. We sat for a long time in what Tashi called "the suffering room" while loud speakers blared at high volume, announcing cancelled flights. Ours was called. Spirits soared, and after boarding the plane, we watched the pilot turn the key to start the engines. Nothing happened. We disembarked and climbed aboard again after a mechanic with a screwdriver made a quick fix.

We took off into dense clouds, which suggested that the opportunity to land in Phaplu had passed.

Now and then a mountain appeared far too close to the plane window as we flew blindly through the clouds, trying to find a clear patch of blue to spiral through. After several steep circles, and to our mixed relief, the pilot announced he was returning to Kathmandu.

The next day we sat again in the suffering room for more than an hour, only to be told that all flights had been cancelled. In the bus on the way back to our hotel, the air could have been cut with a knife. Silent frustration and furrowed brows resulted, and one of the group told me, "We have to have a meeting tonight!" They were considering aborting the trip and heading to the Maldives. We both felt responsible and depressed.

Later that afternoon we led the group to a mountain park at the north end of the city. At the top of the trail was a monastery. On entering the courtyard, we were told by a monk that the monastery was closed because 300 people were in a silent meditation at the time. I said, partly in jest, "Perhaps you could get them to meditate on improving the weather so we can get to our trailhead."

"Ah, but all is changing," he replied.

"But our food and porters are all there waiting for us and we can't fly in these clouds," we told him.

"And that too will change." he replied knowingly.

It was a revelation for the group. By accepting this truth, they were able to view the situation with tolerance. I think we all realized that we are powerless in these situations and must live in the moment.

We had a relaxing hike down the hill, admiring a tall communal swing made of bent bamboo and coconut ropes. It was etched in the light of the setting sun.

The next day, we flew safely to the trailhead and our waiting staff. "All is changing, nothing stays the same," along with Bistarai Ja-nay, became our daily chants.

After thirty visits, our need to discover new areas for trekking was replaced by a desire to return to the peace and solitude of the Solu, one of the first areas we visited in Nepal. Everything was there – high mountains, wilderness unspoiled by tourism, and the spiritual culture of the Sherpas that I so much admired.

I once asked someone when I would know that I had led my last trek. They told me. "You will know – the signs will be there, not by numbers of visits, or age, but instinctively." Sure enough, they were right. I returned home in October 2012, and the feeling was there. It was after a trek that was perfect in so many ways. Our daughter-in-law Catherine and nephew Doug were with me, among others. We explored a holy lake, visited the familiar and treasured school at Ringmu, and ended our trek with two unforgettable days observing the Buddhist celebration of Mani Rimdu at Chiwong Gompa. It all came together in one shining Himalayan experience. Celebrating my 80th birthday in Kathmandu was the icing on the cake.

Would our trekking days ever end? Each year seemed to be better than the last. It was rewarding to know that everyone who travelled with us would experience opportunities for self knowledge and discover a deeper meaning to life. The people, the culture and the mountains of the Himalaya offered this framework.

We are grateful for our trek leaders who shared our dream and for the many trekkers who willingly left their familiar environment to travel with us through the terror and wonder of this magical land.

IN ANY ADVENTURE, WHO PEOPLE ARE CAN BE DETERMINED NOT BY WHAT HAPPENS TO THEM, BUT BY HOW THEY DEAL WITH IT.

– Rosalind MacPhee